WAR IN THE TWILIGHT

A Memoir

by

E. A. Cooper

Dedication

This book is dedicated to my wife, Susan.
She is my strength and inspiration, the love of my life.

A Word From The Author

In an attempt to make my writing clear and crisp, I've followed dictates of Writing 101 and avoided passive words: *as*, *was*, and modifiers ending in *ly*, and those adverbs that end in *ily*. And, in deference to Ernest Hemingway, I've tried to use simple words over harder ones, employ shorter sentences, and use positive language rather than negative wording. However, I might have stumbled a bit when trying to avoid negative wording since I detest war so very much.

Of course, I'm no Hemingway, nor do I want to be, but I admire his writing style. Even my title, *War In The Twilight*, drew inspiration from his title, *Death In The Afternoon*. His novels are considered to be some of the finest ever written. However, unlike Hemingway, I'm not a professional writer. I'm an accidental writer. I just sort of fell into it when I had nothing else better to do. Sorry, it's too late to get your money back, ka-ching!

Also, my memoir is shorter than the typical memoir. That's because it's not about my whole life. For the most part, it's limited to a short time spent overseas, the 10 months or so that I served with the Marines in South Vietnam. Nevertheless, I do hope you'll find my Far East experiences interesting. They were to me. That's why I wrote this memoir. Although, I admit I wouldn't care to relive most of them. Then again, what's life without adventure?

Synopsis

From the demands of rural life to Far East pleasures to horrors of war, *War In The Twilight* is a true-life experience that showcases the triumph of perseverance over adversity.

Rural life may be cherished by many people, I just didn't happen to be one of them. To me farm chores were too repetitious and uninspiring. From my earliest memory, I loved the arts and the creative processes they encompassed. Attending college and immersing myself in the fine arts had long been my dream. Blessed with some artistic talent, I had the good fortune to be offered an art scholarship to a major university. Unfortunately, without additional support, I still lacked sufficient funds needed for ancillary expenses: food, lodging, transportation, and other incidentals.

Determined to leave rural life behind, I had to find a means of subsistence. The search for employment meant that my dream had to be deferred and perhaps never attained. With few skills, I followed the path of a high school classmate and entered military service. In short order, I determined that I did not feel comfortable with the regimen and uniformity of the military. Nevertheless, I had enlisted and had no other practical choice than to make the best of my situation. From that experience, I learned the error of giving in to "sheep instinct."

Assigned to a Far East posting, I found that—due to a global economy favoring America—overseas a variety of personal services and inexpensive merchandise could be had even by low-ranked servicemen like myself. I enjoyed the experience so much that I attempted to extend my one-year assignment for an additional year. Due to my unwillingness to succumb to under-handed extortion by the sergeant who processed extensions, my request didn't see the light-of-day. I had to return to the states. In so doing, I learned a lesson in life's hardscrabble reality: if you want someone to do something for you, at times, no matter how dispiriting, it may be necessary to "grease the wheels."

After returning to military life in America, I missed the personal services and good times that I had come to appreciate overseas. Waiving my rights to remain stateside, I volunteered to return to service in the South Pacific. Failing to keep abreast of news events, I returned to my former posting only to be transferred within a few months to a combat assignment in South Vietnam. I had no choice in the matter. From that disappointment, I learned the value of "keeping up with current events and assessing their probable consequences."

Camped on a barren hill overlooking miles of rice paddies and bamboo thickets, the day's routine repeated day-after-day without much deviation. In time I would come to appreciate the boredom of routine. A surprise attack at midnight by mortar bombardment and, on a later occasion, by a relentless hail of rifle fire from Viet Cong insurgents, made me yearn for a return to complacent days. With some of my fellow servicemen now wounded or dead, I learned to "never take life for granted."

When I returned to the U.S.A., I had but a short time until my discharge from active duty. To my good fortune, and that of other military personnel, Congress had decided to re-instate the "G.I. Bill," providing military veterans with tuition assistance for education and training. Their action made it possible for me to realize my deferred dream of enrolling in college and pursuing the fine arts. From my somewhat circuitous journey, I learned life's most important lesson, "never give up."

Contents

Chapter 1

Prelude to War

I spent almost a year in South Vietnam, and I would like to share that experience with you. First, I will tell you of the events that led me there. I did not plan to travel to the Far East. When I completed high school I wanted to go to college. Despite being offered an art scholarship to a major university, I lacked sufficient funds. Still, I wanted to leave rural life. Without enough money for college, I needed to find a new destination. I had no choice but to change my plans, or at least delay them, while I pursued another option. Money not only determines the mode of travel but also the path one takes.

After reviewing my prospects, I decided to enlist in the military. Like myself, other enlisted Marines that I knew joined the military to escape poverty, dodge a jail sentence, or avoid some other unpleasant experience. I never met a Marine who said he joined for adventure. It seemed to me we were among America's lower-class, its bottom-feeders. Our drill instructors said we were "lower than whale feces," found at the bottom of the ocean. Drill instructors tear you down before they build you up.

The Air Force ranked first in my choices for military service, but they had a year-long waiting list. In a hurry to leave my past behind, I let a schoolmate persuade me to join the U.S. Marine Corps on its "buddy plan." The plan meant we would be allowed to go through boot camp together. The Marine Corps, true to its word, placed us in the same platoon, but we were assigned bunks separated by the full length of the barracks. Thus, we were unable to speak to each other. The Corps discourages its recruits from talking with one another during basic training. Separating us far apart removed any temptation and opportunity we might have had to chit-chat.

I suspect the Marine Corps separates all recruits that enter on the buddy plan. Their conniving strategy taught me a valuable lesson, always be skeptical. I'm not alone in that regard. I recall a song by blues singer, B.B. King. In the song he suspected even his mother might be *jivin'*. Bottom line, I learned to trust no one and to void sheep instinct. I found it better to be a lone wolf than follow along with others. My schoolmate would go on to make a career of the Marines, be assigned to the air wing and be shot down in operation "Desert Storm." Captured, roughed up a bit, and after a short time released, he returned to the States a hero. You might say, I had a different compass.

After completing basic training, I reported to my first duty assignment, the Third Marine Division, 3rd Force Service Regiment, Supply Company, stationed at Camp Sukiran in Okinawa. At that time, Sukiran, an Army Base, provided the Marine Corps with a few barracks and administrative buildings for supply operations. Less regimented than Marine Corps bases, Sukiran had open-gate liberty, meaning there were no sentries at the gates—easy come, easy go. Years later, when the Japanese took over governance of the island, the base's name changed to Camp Zukiran. Still later, when the

Army vacated the base, leaving Marines in charge, the Marine Corps changed the base's name to Camp Foster. With hard-ass Marines in charge, open-gate liberty became a thing of the past. It seems to me that overtime most things change but not always for the better.

My memories of the island date back to the early 1960s. At that time, Okinawa's economy still suffered from ill effects of WWII. To bolster its economy, the island became tax-exempt. Goods and services were abundant and cheap. Inexpensive tailored-made suits and shirts could be had in the parking lot behind our barracks. You selected material from samples in a salesman's car trunk, and you were measured on the spot. Within a week or so you received your custom-tailored clothing. I recall that an eight-place setting of Noritake china cost only fifty dollars and could be shipped home at little expense. A fellow Marine I knew claimed to have bought a Rolex Oyster Perpetual watch for only sixty-eight bucks. Whether used or not, I don't know, but it appeared to be new and authentic.

Okinawans, for meager wages, provided a variety of personal services. For example, we had an augmented mess. We each paid fifty cents on payday, every two weeks. For that sum Okinawans performed our mess duties, thus relieving low-rated Marines from the thirty days of mess duty we were required to perform each year. Also, after we left the barracks to report to our work stations, Okinawan young men arrived. For fifty cents a payday, they kept our boots and shoes shined, whatever we left under our bunks. After completing their task, they left before we returned. We only saw them on pay days. Another fifty cents paid for a gardener, who, among other duties, picked up all of our cigarette butts. Young Okinawan females, that we called "laundry girls," kept our uniforms and civilian clothes clean, pressed, and starched for about five dollars per payday. Dry-cleaning cost an extra dollar or two.

Being a Pfc, I only earned $42 per two-week pay period, which included nine dollars a month overseas pay. That's a paltry $21 per week. Yet, in Okinawa my meager salary allowed me to enjoy many personal services, and I still had money left over for basic essentials and off-base pleasures.

However, to my regret, my money always ran out a few days before payday. Without money, I spent my time watching TV in the barracks' recreation room. I remember tuning in Japan's favorite TV show, the American western, *Bonanza*. Dubbed over, the show's actors spoke in high-pitched Japanese dialogue. I found that amusing. In fairness, I suspect my southern accent would be amusing to them.

After-hours liberty couldn't have been better. On base, mixed drinks in the Marine's enlisted club were 10 cents each, a pack of cigarettes only twelve. Off base, in towns and villages, prices were a bit higher, 50 cents for a beer and 65 cents for a mixed drink. To their advantage, the off-base clubs had friendly bar girls. If you bought them drinks, they would sit beside you, chat, tell jokes, and dance. The drinks they ordered were full-priced but watered down. That way they could drink all night without getting drunk and make money until your wallet emptied or you decided to leave. Still, if they got to know you and liked you, they might be persuaded to take you to their apartment after closing time.

The apartments housing bar girls consisted of only two or three small rooms. In the front room, they heated and cooked on a small grill, called a *shichirin*. To avoid noxious fumes, they used a white, Japanese charcoal called, *binchotan*, created for indoor use. I remember that the special charcoal gave off little or no smoke. Once, during a winter month, I accompanied two bar girls to an apartment they shared. We sat on the floor next to their warm grill while we chatted and munched on cubes of pickled turnip roots. I recall that simple experience with fondness.

The bar girls often had an impoverished home life. When they started working, they had to borrow money from the club owners for rent, furnishings, essentials, and any money needed back home. Earning a low wage, they remained in debt for years. They were able to earn a little extra pay, based on the number of drinks their customers bought. Still, they were like indentured servants, similar to mill workers in America's Deep South, always in debt to the company store. It would take years for most of them to settle their debt. Lucky ones had military boyfriends who paid off the money they owed, so they could marry and move to the states.

In Okinawa, many bars were within walking distance from military bases. After work, Marines headed out like columns of ants in search of a good time. In the villages, a short-time affair could be had for two dollars, an all-night tryst for five—at least that's what I heard. For servicemen with morals of rabid billy goats, Okinawa earned the reputation of being the best overseas assignment.

Once when bar-hopping off base, I had a few too many drinks and, having an over-night pass, decided to spend the night in local lodging. I woke up the next morning hung-over with only minutes to return to base before roll call. I dressed in a hurry and hailed the first cab I saw. I arrived too late. Roll call, conducted at 0500 in the barracks' parking lot, had ended. My fellow Marines were now inside having breakfast in the barracks' mess hall. I entered the mess hall still in civilian clothes. I sought out the duty NCO to turn in my over-night pass and liberty card. The NCO looked surprised to see me still in civvies.

"Are you just coming in?" he asked.

"No, I work in civilian clothes," I answered with a sarcastic tone.

I thought my absence had been detected. Unbeknownst to me, at roll call someone in the ranks answered "here" in my behalf, and I had been counted present. If I had changed into my work uniform before entering the mess hall, the duty NCO would have thought I had just forgotten to turn in my pass and liberty card, no big deal. Everything would have been fine. Yet, I let my alligator mouth overload my jaybird ass. The corporal remained calm, and without looking up, notated my late arrival in the company log book. I now faced non-judicial punishment for missing formation and being AWOL.

At my office hours hearing, my company commander restricted me to the base for two weeks. In true Marine Corps tradition, lights went out at 2200—and so did I. Being on restriction, I had no pass, but Camp Sukiran had no sentries. Slipping off base in the dark presented no problem. MPs, while on patrol in bar and nightclub areas, would check IDs and liberty cards when an altercation or some other disturbance occurred. Otherwise, they tended not to bother, so I took a minor risk going off base. Yet, if caught the consequences would be severe.

Each and every night while on restriction, I walked off base to a near-by bar. On one such occasion, in walked the Non-Commissioned

Officer-In-Charge of my work station along with the Officer-In-Charge, a warrant officer. Hoping to avoid detection, I lowered my head and stared down at my shoes. Of course, that silly ploy did not work, and they were soon standing beside me. The warrant officer, aware I had been assigned restriction, asked if I would be returning to base.

I answered, "Yes, sir. I do every night."

The two of them shook their heads in dismay and left the bar. The next day at work, I asked the NCOIC why the warrant officer did not take action against me. If he had, it would have resulted in yours truly being sentenced to time in the brig. He replied that the warrant officer said I reminded him of himself when he had been my age. Realizing how close I came to serious punishment, I decided to mend my ways. I served out the remainder of my military service in exemplary fashion, receiving nominations for both "Marine of the Month" and "Marine of the Quarter."

I served the normal 13-month tour of duty in Okinawa and rotated back to the states. Four months prior to leaving, I submitted a written request to the company sergeant to extend my tour in Okinawa for another year. A fellow Marine told me that I would need to slip the sergeant $30 to ensure my request got approved. On principle, I refused to follow that advice. I should have listened. My request never got processed let alone approved. When questioned, the sergeant denied receiving it. Lesson learned: If you want a smooth ride, you need to grease the wheels.

After returning to the states, I missed all the personal services and cheap goods available in Okinawa. Without delay, I volunteered to return. Sometimes it's unfortunate when you get what you want. Just five months into my second tour of duty on the island, the Third Division got orders to transfer to South Vietnam. The Third Division had been assigned to Okinawa since the end of the war of the Pacific. I had no reason to suspect that it might not be there forever. I had just turned 21 and had become rather fond of drinking, smoking, and chasing skirts. Needless to say, I hadn't been keeping up with current events. I knew very little about Vietnam and its political instability.

In the early 1960s, there had been news coverage regarding political unrest in South Vietnam, so I can't claim to be unaware of the turmoil, just naive to its possible consequences. I recall the visit to America made in 1963 by Madam Nhu. She served in the role of Vietnam's first lady. Her husband was the brother of President Ngo Dinh Diem, a bachelor. The Diems were Catholics and treated Buddhists, followers of the region's most popular religion, in a bad way. Trying to force better treatment for Buddhists, U.S. President John F. Kennedy imposed economic sanctions on Vietnam.

In retaliation, Madam Nhu, a rather outspoken person, accused President Kennedy of being soft on communism. Kennedy's support of the Diem regime soon weakened. That's about all I remember about the matter. A typical male teenager, my attention focused more on the photo of Madam Nhu's daughter, Le Thuy. She had accompanied her mother on the trip to America. I considered her to be attractive. I blame my testosterone for diverting my attention from serious news.

It's difficult for me to admit, but I set myself up for transfer to a war zone. Having completed a tour of duty overseas exempted me from being reassigned outside of the United States. Yet, the memory of good times and personal services in Okinawa fueled my desire to return. I waived my rights to remain state-side in order to transfer back. In the military, one doesn't volunteer for service in a country. You volunteer to serve in whatever unit is assigned to that country. Thus, when the Third Division transferred to South Vietnam, I had no choice but to go with them. That's how I ended up in a war zone. The lure of Okinawa's cheap goods and personal services led me to it. From that experience, I learned the value of staying abreast of current affairs and the need to weigh possible outcomes.

My tour of duty in South Vietnam began in July 1965 and ended in

May of 1966. My memoir is not reflective of the Vietnam War in general. Service in a war zone is different for different troops. That's one reason my memoir is not a typical "blood and guts" war story. The extent to which you dealt with or witnessed carnage depended upon various factors: when you served, where you served, the outfit you served with, your primary job, and how often you served, etc. My time spent in South Vietnam amounted to a pleasure cruise when compared to that of most other veterans. Bottom-line, in war there's no one size fits all.

When writing this memoir, I used a lighthearted style of writing with an occasional attempt at humor. I can understand if some readers, who may have lost a loved one or a close friend to the war or had one injured, would not be enamored with my casual approach. I meant no disrespect. It's a writing style that allowed me to address a time and place that otherwise I would not have cared to revisit.

With regret, my memoir omits the contributions of female personnel. The only reason for such bias is that I never served with females. Once when visiting a wounded comrade, I did see female, military nurses at the hospital in Da Nang. I only saw them in passing, and I did not speak with them. Times have changed. I'm aware that today some females in the Army have qualified for infantry duty and for several years have held leadership positions. I'm proud of the progress they've made against tough odds. I have no doubt that females will continue to excel in the ranks. I wish them well, but, again, I did not serve with them.

Another point I wish to make is that our troops are recruited from the general population. Alas, the military inherits a representative share of malingers and other unsavory types. This may be contrary to the perception of our nation's populace, who worship our boys in uniform, but it's the reason we have the Uniform Code of Military Justice (UCMJ), court-martial procedures, and military stockades and brigs. Life is a mixture of good and bad. When you're lucky, the good far outweighs the negative in life. It's no different in the military. Among the honorable troops, there are unsavory types. Over time, most get rooted out, but there are some that manage to slide under the radar. I know because I served with them. I suspect they can be found in every rank.

I worked in supply, but all Marines are trained as infantrymen, so I had duties that required the use of my rifle and other weaponry. I can't claim to be a good shot. We fired for qualification each year. On the Marine Corps's 500-yard rifle ranges, I only qualified "marksman," Below marksman are those shooters ranked "unqualified." Once I fired on the Army's 300-yard rifle range at Fort Benning, GA. I qualified "sharpshooter," a qualification above marksman but below "expert."

To my good fortune, prior to transferring to South Vietnam, I had been assigned to 3rd Tank Battalion, Headquarters & Service Company. Our camp had so much fire power on its defensive perimeter that the enemy, for the most part, tended to leave us alone and stayed out of our area. Notice, I said, "for the most part." When the Viet Cong did infiltrate our area of defense, they remained out of sight and left not long after being engaged by our troops. Nevertheless, VC sniper fire remained a constant concern.

Tank companies that operated in the field engaged in firefights on a more frequent basis. Their mission required them to seek out trouble. I did my best to avoid it. There were other military personnel who, after completing their tour of duty, volunteered to return. I don't know why. I read that Napoleon said, "Men are led by baubles." If that's true, maybe they thought by returning they would get another medal to pin on their uniform or perhaps earn a promotion.

I didn't care to be a hero. Many heroes are killed. I suppose I'd be considered an anti-hero. I didn't even care to be promoted. A promotion meant more pay but also more responsibility. Leadership sucks. It requires you to do things in a responsible way and set examples for others to follow. That's a bit too much *goody-two shoes* for me. I didn't want to be looked up to or down upon. I just wanted to be left alone, do my time and get out.

The few fond memories that I do have of Vietnam are from nighttime guard duty. In the glow of the night's moon, I admired the shimmer of light reflected off terraced rice paddies and silhouettes of bamboo and palm trees. Quite often, I became transfixed in the twilight's scenic beauty. I would forget that the purpose of my assignment had to do with spotting enemy troop movement. And, if attacked, to provide the initial defense of our camp until troops sleeping in the tent area could awaken and join the fight. For me, the twilight often cast a spell, aiding my desire to escape thoughts of war. During my stay in South Vietnam, I enjoyed the twilight hours more than any other time of the day or night.

Our involvement in Vietnam lasted just over 20 years, and despite the best efforts of the U.S. Military, the war ended—after the deaths of over 58,000 U.S. troops—with our hasty withdrawal in 1973. The last few Americans remaining in South Vietnam were airlifted out in 1975. Within two years after we evacuated, the communist forces we fought against entered Saigon and took over governance of the country. Over 40 years later, when I started writing this memoir, communists still ruled Vietnam.

Hanoi had been the capital of North Vietnam during the war and the place where American POWs were incarcerated and tortured. The confinement facility had been dubbed, in a nod to dark humor, the "Hanoi Hilton." Americans now vacation in communist-ruled Vietnam. Today, there is an actual Hilton hotel in Hanoi, the Hilton Hanoi Opera. The hotel is so named because of its location near the site of an old opera house, and to distance its name from past memories. My Lai, the site of a terrible massacre during the war, maintains its name, but now hosts a theme park with carnival rides.

American franchise restaurants, including McDonald's, Starbucks, and KFC now operate in Da Nang. I've read that Vietnamese malls sell Levi jeans and Converse tennis shoes, and throughout Vietnam, iPads are popular items. When I served in South Vietnam, I remember noise coming from hamlets that sounded like villagers sending signals by beating on large segments of bamboo. Today I suppose they use smartphones.

Several years ago, I purchased a jacket in a clothing store located in the southern United States. I didn't notice until I got home that its label read, "Made in Vietnam." I don't wear it anymore, due to my son taking a liking to it, with *taking* being the operative word. Nevertheless, for me the purloined jacket is a testament to the absurdity of war. One day you're fighting people, a few years later you're buying clothes from them.

Well, enough of my incessant grumbling about the futility of war. Nobody listens anyway. We always seem eager for a fight. Ignoring lessons learned in South Vietnam, we have intervened in Iran, Iraq, and Afghanistan. We seem incapable of defeating guerrilla insurgents. Yet, we keep engaging them. I'm starting to think it may not be so much about winning. It may have more to do with how long our government can keep the war enterprise thriving.

So, where to next? Your guess might be better than mine. Perhaps we should ask one of the many defense contractors that provides our government with military material, equipment, services, and other essentials. I suspect they might know the answer, or, at least, I imagine that they are hard at work searching for it. I doubt they'll rest until they know. After all, they do have a vested interest in America's on-going war involvement. It's how they generate their profits and satisfy their stockholders. It's the American way, capitalism at its finest.

Note: We recently ended our military involvement in Afghanistan, our longest war to date, much the same as we did in South Vietnam and with much the same result. To quote Yogi Berra: "It's deja vu all over again." We never learn.

Chapter 2

Departure and Landing

When the order came for all units of the Third Division to ship to Vietnam, I had just run over my foot with a pallet jack, not an easy thing to do. The pain caused me to limp. I requested to have my foot seen at our dispensary. The officer-in-charge of the supply shop where I worked didn't offer any sympathy. He ordered me, in no uncertain terms, to go and return without delay. He didn't want anyone in his command left behind. I think he believed my accident to be deliberate, a way for me to avoid shipping off to a war zone. He gave me too much credit. I wish I had been that smart. I would have run over both feet.

Members of 3rd Tank Battalion boarded the *LSD Alamo* in Naha, Okinawa, July of 1965. We had a forecast of a calm sea and smooth sailing. Still, the voyage came with a downside, hot climate and no breeze. From contrasts like smooth sailing and sweltering heat, I learned that good often comes with bad and vice versa. Despite the smooth sailing, the hot weather spoiled the trip. Going below deck gave no relief. Quarters were cramped, so Marines retreated up rather than down in search of elbow room and fresh air. With so many Marines crowding the top deck, it became difficult to jockey for position in what little shade the ship's upper structure provided. Meal times were the only break in the voyage's monotony but gave no relief from the crowded situation or the heat.

Midway between Okinawa and South Vietnam we passed a Russian vessel, flying its hammer & sickle ensign. We took photos, and I'm guessing they took photos, too. The cold war had not ended, and seeing the Russian flag gave me an eerie feeling. I had doubts that the passing so close at sea had been coincidental. I suspected the Russians were monitoring our troop movement. At any rate, both ships continued on their way and soon lost sight of each other. After six days at sea, we off-loaded on Red Beach 2 just a few miles north of Da Nang. We were told we were an advanced party, clearing the way for others to follow. Prior to disembarking, we were issued live ammo, a clear indication that serious business lie ahead.

Unlike other military branches of service, that store all of its weapons in an armory, the Marine Corps required us to keep our rifles in our possession. Not only intended for use in combat, we also used our rifles in the execution of close-order drill, a practice of precision and uniformity. However, we were only issued ammunition when on the firing range, until now. In preparation for our invasion, we were issued ammo for the four magazines we wore on our cartridge belts, 80 rounds total. We would be issued more if and when hostilities required it, including grenades and other specialized weapons.

We were warned that Viet Cong guerrilla fighters didn't wear uniforms and recruited old men, women, and children. Unlike wars of previous years, you couldn't rely on clothing, gender, age, or even disposition to identify the enemy. When on daytime patrol of surrounding area, the villager who greeted you with a smile might shoot at you during the night. A young kid, trained by VC, might walk up next to you with a grenade in hand and pull the pin. The inability to recognize the enemy made our task all the more difficult, but no one ever said war would be easy.

The *LSD Alamo* maneuvered its stern to the beach. Then it opened its well dock, so that troops, supplies, and equipment, including M48A3 Patton tanks and M67 Zippo tanks, could disembark. Hitting the beach, I imagined myself in a John Wayne movie, charging forward like Marines did in the "Sands of Iwo Jima." The absence of background music ruined my illusion.

A fellow Marine told me that a Vietnamese, NBC film crew recorded our beach landing, but I didn't see them. Fearing that we might be met by hostile fire, I riveted my attention to the immediate front. Before the year ended, I learned to look forward, sideways, and to the rear. You never knew from which direction the enemy might come or when. And, then it happened, out of nowhere a Vietnamese lad popped up on the beach. In each hand he held—an unopened bottle of *Coca-Cola*.

"Hey, Joe. You want to buy a Coke?" he asked.

I thought to myself, *Damn, he speaks better English than I do.*

Being from the Deep South, I spoke a bit slower and softer. I guessed that the young boy learned English from someone who spoke with a General American accent. Probably an officer, a military adviser. American advisers had been in South Vietnam for several years. The irony of my encountering an English-speaking, Vietnamese youngster and Coke-Cola being available in a war zone, did not escape me. To say the least, it made mockery of our "advanced party" designation.

With nothing but sand to shield us, we formed a defensive perimeter on the beach, waiting for the attack that never came. In all likelihood, our leaders were just buying time to put their heads together and try to figure out the shortest route to our new base of operations. We were all eager to get somewhere before nightfall. We needed time to get a lay of the land and dig-in. Even combat-ready Marines feel uneasy in the dark.

When ordered, our troops gathered into their respective units and soon boarded trucks to head to our new campsite a few miles southwest of Da Nang. Every Marine departed, except two others and myself. We were left to stay on the beach to guard several stacks of C-rations. We were to protect the food supply against theft, until transport trucks, now filled with troops, could return the next day.

At first, it seemed like a good assignment. We were camped on the beach. If we liked, we could take a dip in the ocean. We had plenty to eat and smoke, as much as we wanted, and no one to order us around. And then, it started to get dark. That's when it hit me. Sometimes reality can ruin a good day.

What if there are Viet Cong in the area? There are only three of us. We could be killed. Better put out my cigarette. Don't want to make myself a target in the dark, I reasoned to myself.

Perhaps, worried is the more accurate word. My worries were eased a little when we received a surprise visit by a military chaplain. Like the Vietnamese lad peddling Coca-Cola, he seemed to appear out of nowhere. Stationed at the Da Nang Air Base, the chaplain said he heard about our landing and came to offer a few words of encouragement. Why he waited until dusk to make the trip puzzled me. Perhaps, he had been busy saving the souls of others. Undeterred that he arrived late and found only three Marines on the beach, he decided to share his thoughts anyway. Preachers are like that. Only, I think he tailored his message to the reprobates he found. I'm told that most preachers have a divine radar for identifying non-believers and transgressors.

"Men, I've completed my tour and will be headed home in a few days, but, before I go, I can tell you Marines how to win this war. First, you round up 50 of the healthiest, young, Vietnamese males and females, and you put them 50 miles offshore on an aircraft carrier. Next, conduct a scorched-earth campaign. Burn and kill everything and everybody from one end of South Vietnam to the other. Once you've completed that mission, go out and sink that fucking ship."

After delivering his inspiring message, the chaplain stood up and faded back into the dark.

I thought, *He must be one of those baptized in fire Holy Rollers.*

We had already eaten to our stomachs' content, but since we could get away with it, we decided to open up some more C-rations. We only ate the desserts and smoked some more of the ten-year plus old cigarettes. The smokes in my ration box were Lucky Strikes in a green wrapper with the iconic bulls-eye target logo. On the bottom it read, "L-S-M-F-T: Lucky Strike means fine tobacco." I remembered that slogan from my childhood, which may have been when my cigarettes had been packaged. It's surprising how long some products will last when sealed air-tight.

With the chaplain's message fresh on our minds, we considered staying awake in shifts, but we were tired and decided to chance it. After all, what were the odds that Viet Cong guerrillas, with an unobstructed view, would notice six-foot high stacks of cardboard boxes sitting on a beach? And, there's no way the pup tent we stretched from the tops of two of the stacks to shelter us from the morning dew would draw attention to the fact that people were encamped there. I guess we were hoping the Viet Cong would think the boxes just washed ashore. I never said we were smart. After all, we were Marines—and reprobates.

Chapter 3

Hill 34

The military transport trucks arrived on the beach mid-morning. We loaded the C-rations and climbed aboard the back of one of the trucks. It had fold-down seating made of hard strips of wood that exaggerated every bump in the road, and there were lots of bumps. Riding through the countryside, it seemed that rice paddies were everywhere. On the edge of the paddies, bamboo thickets shaded a scattering of hamlets. A few main roads were paved, but most roads were dirt ones and quite dusty. Well, that is until the arrival of the monsoon season, then mud ruled the day.

About seven and a half miles southwest of Da Nang, near the village of Phonc Bac, we reached Hill 34, named by its height in meters. The hill reached the apex of its height at its southern edge, overlooking a winding river and expansive fields of rice paddies we called "Happy Valley." Since we placed our tent area further back from front of the hill, our living quarters could not be seen by the enemy to the south of us. The hill had compacted soil made harder by embedded granite rock. The bamboo thickets to our immediate east and west hid small hamlets of two to four families each, maybe a few more. To the front and bottom of our hill, palm trees and bamboo thickets bordered the rice paddies allowing villagers to pass before us unseen. To our immediate south, the rice paddies of Happy Valley extended for 50 miles or more. The paddies were interspersed with bamboo thickets and other growth that hid additional hamlets from our view.

An artillery company nearby to the north and rear of our campsite, whenever directed to do so by a forward observer, blasted away with their two large 155 howitzers and several smaller 105 artillery pieces. The artillery rounds sailed up and over our encampment and traveled for miles far south of us. We were warned that artillery sometimes had *short rounds*, defective ammo that failed to travel far and might strike our camp. You tried not to think about the things you had no control over, but each time the artillery blasted away, you wondered if this would be the day you saw a bright flash and heard angels singing or maybe the devil laughing. After weeks had past, you were able to put it out of mind. Such matters were best left to fate.

A forward observer, with his periscope-like binoculars, would set up at the south end of our hill over-looking the valley below. Whatever he viewed exceeded the range of my vision, but every so often he picked up his field phone and called in coordinates, and then the artillery let loose and rounds whizzed overhead followed by puffs of smoke miles away. You wondered what he had seen, and if the explosions killed enemy or had collateral damage, the death of innocents. Yes, war is hell.

To the immediate north of our camp, between us and the artillery unit, a platoon of AmTracs were clustered. The amphibious, tracked vehicles had the traditional role of ferrying troops ashore from warships. In Vietnam, they were repurposed to transport troops through the jungles and rice fields into the thick of battle. They also retrieved tanks that had become stuck in mud, a frequent occurrence during the monsoon season. For that reason, tanks tended to stay on roadways and perform like mobile artillery.

AmTrac crewmen liked to adorn their vehicles with amusing renderings, similar to the drawings on WWII bombers. Each era is different, and the Marine Corps, due to its conservative leadership, would not allow drawings of curvaceous women like those painted on aircraft. I still remember the AmTrac with *Made By Mattel* lettered on its front sides. For benefit of those that might not know, Mattel is a toy manufacturer. Another read, *Gone With The Wind*, the title of a famous American novel and movie. Tanks, on the other hand, had an oddly shaped surface that did not lend itself to such creativity. I did hear of one tank that had a large bat stenciled on its search-light lens.

Our battalion commander utilized an AmTrac, since they were made of thick steel, for his battalion headquarters. Out of caution, he had the vehicle buried to its top, offering him protection lacked by the rest of us. He assured us that if we were ever over-run, he'd call an artillery strike directly onto our camp. Safe inside his buried headquarters, he would survive anything other than a direct hit.

How considerate of him, I thought. *If the enemy didn't kill us, he would.*

An Ontos unit defended our perimeter's west flank. The light-weight, tracked vehicle came equipped with six 106mm guns capable of knocking down a wall. It also had a .30 caliber machine gun for anti-infantry use. In addition, a *beehive* round that unleashed 10,000 steel *flechettes* (darts) had been developed for the 106mm guns. Re-loaded from the outside, it became known as a "shoot-and-scoot" weapon. They would fire and then run for cover in order to re-load in safety. By the way, *Ontos* is Greek, meaning "thing," an apt description of the small vehicle.

Headquarters & Service Battalion had three tank companies: Alpha, Bravo, and Charlie. Alpha Company had a search and destroy mission, patrolling throughout Happy Valley, the area to our south. Bravo Company received an assignment south of Da Nang on the coast. Due to over crowding at the Da Nang Air Base, a Marine helicopter unit, MAG 16, constructed an airfield near the beach and needed the protective support of a tank company. Charlie Company provided fire power for Marines stationed south of Happy Valley at Chu Lai. Our Battalion Headquarters provided the support services the three tank companies needed in order to remain operational and effective.

On Hill 34, the battalion's company office, maintenance, and other support operations were housed. Personnel included supply clerks, tank mechanics, communication specialists, medical corpsmen, cooks, various support troops, and a few tank crewman. The tank crewmen were assigned to the three tanks spaced apart on our perimeter. When we first arrived to our campsite, I worked in the Shop Stores section issuing small items needed by units to function properly. A short time later, after a tragic event, I changed jobs and became a fiscal clerk. I coined the title, "Battalion Exchequer." Since neither a promotion or pay raise came with the new job, I compensated by giving myself a fancy title.

Not limited to performing clerical tasks, about every third night I stood perimeter guard duty. Likewise, I went out on occasional day-time patrol of the local area. I also participated in night-ambush along the nearby river. After completion of such assignments, Marines still reported to work, but we were allowed to arrive an hour or so late. Being hung-over from lack of sleep, did not seem to concern our superiors. Assignments tend to pile up in a war zone. Perhaps that's why the Marine Corps, when it comes to participation in combat, is an equal opportunity employer.

Perhaps, the Corps failed to alter my cynical attitude. I always thought, if ordered to charge a machine-gun nest head-on, I would carry out the order in a different manner. It seemed to me that a low-crawling envelopment made more sense, safer anyway. I would claim that I misunderstood the specifics of the order. I never cared much for lock-step mentality. I resisted the best efforts of my drill sergeants to forge me into becoming an unquestioning, fighting robot. I had a brain of my own, and I intended to use it.

While in boot camp, whenever we were required to reply in unison, "Yes, sir," I always said "Yes, cur." Of course, no one heard me, except myself. Maybe a bit too passive-aggressive, but such gambits helped me to maintain my independence of mind. Still, I knew that legal orders, should be followed without hesitation, if for no other reason than to stay out of trouble. However, I added my own caveat. The orders had to be logical. I didn't intend to die following an ill-advised order, so that some higher-ranked Marine could be promoted or awarded another medal. I would rather be thrown in the brig and live to *view* another day. I did mean to say view rather than fight. Fight is a last resort in my vocabulary, to be avoided if at all possible.

In truth, I had no business joining the Marines. My personality favored fine arts. I really didn't care for military matters or actions, no matter how much justified by world conflict. Perhaps, I should have been a conscientious objector. When we invaded South Vietnam, I couldn't help but question why we were there. I heard that our mission had to do with being a part of a perimeter of military units that defended the Da Nang Air Base. We were to prevent the enemy from coming within mortar range of the air base or slipping in enough VC guerrillas to mount an attack.

Beyond that, I had no idea of the big picture. I assumed we were supporting South Vietnam's dictatorial government in order to prevent a communist takeover and to keep the "domino effect" from occurring— the collapse of one country leading to the collapse of others. However, it seemed to me that the regimes we often supported were oppressive to their own people and treacherous to their political opponents. One such example: Haiti's, Papa Doc Duvalier and his notorious henchmen, the Tonton Macoutes. The U.S. supported Papa Doc's regime for many years. To me, communism seemed a lesser evil. I would have bet money that the residents of Haiti's slums would have preferred it.

Still, no matter the reason, the fact remained, we were seven and a half miles southwest of the city of Da Nang, encamped on a barren hill embedded with granite rock and overlooking bamboo thickets and rice paddies that extended for several miles. The other outposts were nearby but not in sight, probably to keep us from shooting one another. Having started the fourth year of my four-year term of active duty, I believed if I could avoid being shot or struck by shrapnel and make it home alive, my life would take a turn for the better. During the past month or so, our government had reinstated the GI Bill. The bill provided money to military veterans for college tuition. That meant I could now go to college and have a more promising future.

From the time we arrived, returning to the states, with my body and faculties intact, became my top priority. "Safety First" became my motto. I would do whatever I had to do, whenever ordered to do it. Of course, I might drag my feet a bit, and that might be an understatement. Above all, I remained mindful of the need to be ever so careful if I expected to remain alive and injury free. The military had its mission, and I had my mine. And, to quote the immortal words of Rudyard Kipling . . . "and never the twain shall meet."

Chapter 4

Setting Up Camp

Due to a lack of supplies, setting up camp became an ongoing work-in-progress. At first, we slept on the ground, nestled in sleeping bags. Despite it being mid-summer, the nights would get a bit chilly, and the sleeping bags were comfortable and held the cold at bay. The Marine Corps doesn't like for its troops to be too comfortable, afraid they might get soft. After a few weeks, we were advised that the sleeping bags were designated cold-weather gear. Being in a semi-tropical zone, we didn't qualify for them, and they were taken from us.

In their place, we were issued the military's traditional folding cots and a thin, wool blanket. The stiff cots weren't comfortable. Enterprising Vietnamese learned of our discomfort and saw a way to make a dollar. They sold us cotton-padded comforters tailored to the size of our cots. The comforters served like a thin mattresses and provided some cushion. Also, the Marine Corps did not issue pillows, but once again entrepreneurial Vietnamese came to our rescue with small-sized pillows that gave some relief from neck strain. Likewise, Vietnamese provided laundry service. For a small fee, they would wash and press our clothing. Although, at times the clothes had a slight tint suggesting they might have been washed in a rice paddy.

Perhaps our biggest problem had been arriving without lumber. After weeks had past, a group of Seabees came to our rescue with lumber and plywood and constructed the framework for our general purpose tents. The tents were 18' by 36.' Each housed a dozen troops. During the summer, we kept the canvas sides rolled up to keep from baking ourselves. We appreciated the tents most during the annual monsoon season. However, the tents had to be painted with tar wherever they touched wood framing, or rain would seep through. I know this to be true first-hand. I had the privilege of painting our tent with tar, including climbing on the very top of it to seal the canvas where it touched rafters.

The Seabees used the plywood they brought with them for constructing flooring. We appreciated having floors in our tents, but everyday the flooring collected dirt or, when it rained, mud. Our tents did not require waxing and polishing like barracks back in the states, but the plywood floor needed to be swept out every morning before work. At the time, being a low-ranked lance/corporal, I did more than my share of broom duty. I never complained about it though.

I thought, *It's home away from home, might as well keep it clean.*

About halfway through my tour in South Vietnam, I received a promotion to full corporal, a non-commissioned officer rank. My days of sweeping ended. I might not of had to sweep anymore, but I did help with stacking sandbags about two and a half to three feet high along the sides of our tents. The sandbags were meant to protect us from shrapnel if mortars hit nearby. The hill had more than its fair share of embedded granite rock, so mortars striking our hard terrain, instead of sending shrapnel upward in a cone spiral, tended to send shrapnel spread out at ground level. Of course, sandbags wouldn't stop mortar rounds raining down on the tent's canvas roof. Thus, we depended upon luck to protect us from direct hits. During my stay, our luck held out and our tent remained intact.

The tent area occupied the north backside of the hill. We were invisible to enemy activity to the south, the area most vulnerable to incoming fire. Employing a mechanical ditch-digger, a few trenches were dug near the tent area. The trenches were intended to give us a place of refuge if caught by surprise while out in the open. Our hilltop landscape had no trees, no grass, no flowers. Still, even on barren rock, the tent area provided our basic requirement, a place to sleep, a nighttime refuge.

Regarding protection for our camp, we had perimeter trenches connecting our defensive bunkers, but there didn't seem to be any rush to complete construction of the bunkers. Each of the them housed a machine gun which members of our platoon took turns manning from early evening hours to daybreak. I assumed that our leadership felt that the presence of three tanks and the Ontos unit would discourage the enemy from attacking during the day. The tanks were equipped with a M36 90mm gun, which I suppose most civilians would call a canon. In addition, each tank came armed with a coaxial .30-caliber Browning and a .50-caliber Browning M2 machine gun mounted onto its turret. The tank crews, consisting of three men per tank, stayed on guard 24 hours a day. At night, two crewmen would be on guard duty while the third man slept in the driver's seat or tried to. They would rotate positions every few hours.

With our bunkers not fully completed, we were vulnerable to the life-threatening effects of a mortar barrage, the kind of attack where the enemy may or may not intend to invade with troops. Perhaps we hadn't yet acquired enough sand bags or enough sand needed to fill the bags. I did not know the reason the bunkers were still uncompleted. I did know we lacked the wood necessary to construct tops for the bunkers. Without tops our bunkers had no protection from direct hits. In addition, we had one bunker without sandbags for its backside. That omission would cost the life of one of my fellow Marines.

Some of our officers where combat veterans and should have known of the potential peril we faced. Maybe they did, but they didn't consult or communicate much with lower-ranked types. Still, an explanation would have been nice, but I suppose it wouldn't have made any difference. One officer did express remorse later on when tragedy struck. In a mortar attack, we had several Marines wounded and a few killed. One of the deceased Marines, killed while on duty in a bunker, the one without a back or top, worked for the officer.

The officer in question took action to acquire the needed sandbags and lumber. I heard it said that the wood came from the Air Force base at Da Nang. I don't know what deal made the acquisition possible, but

I do know that a case of Ka-bar knifes came up missing during our supply inventory. After that, our bunkers were soon completed. The uncompleted bunkers had reminded me of the quote by Alfred Lord Tennyson, "Ours not to reason why, ours but to do and die." Yeah, right. Screw that. .

Chapter 5

Daily Routine

In a rush to depart from Okinawa, some dim-witted Marine forgot to bring the bugle. Instead of musical reveille at 0500, the duty NCO came through each tent shaking and waking troops. For enlisted Marines reading this memoir, Mickey's big hand pointed to twelve, and his little hand pointed to five. Yeah, I know, that's an old joke, but I couldn't resist using it. Only Marines and former Marines are allowed to tell jokes about other Marines without a fight breaking out. Despite my four plus years of active duty, two tours of duty overseas, and a bit of combat experience, I seldom joke about Marines, not to their face anyway.

The morning's first order of business, getting dressed in "utilities," a Marine's working uniform. It's called "fatigues" by the U.S. Army— and most normal people. Once dressed, a cold water shave came next. I collected the water in my helmet from the "water buffalo," a portable water-tank parked just outside our tent. With unheated water and no shaving cream, for me the daily shaving requirement became an ordeal. You can get by with a neatly trimmed mustache in the Marine Corps, but the Corps doesn't allow beards, so the morning shave could not be avoided, ouch.

Only those Marines coming off night-time guard duty or river ambush were allowed to take a morning shower. The rest of us didn't have the time anyway. We had to hurry to work. Not being able to take an early shower didn't hurt my feelings, since the water in the shower's over-head tank wasn't heated. Later in the day, after work hours, the water would be somewhat warmer thanks to the benefit of the sun's rays on the metal container. The shower had a surrounding structure made from roofing tin, so at least it offered some privacy. The Marine Corps seldom gave any concern to privacy. I supposed the tin structure had been built so that villager's eyes wouldn't be damaged by seeing Marines in the nude.

Nearby, we had a five-hole outhouse. After a morning whiz or poop, shaving, getting dressed, and sweeping out our living quarters, one could head to the mess tent. A stainless steel mess tray, with divided depressions to keep different foods separate, held our morning ration of scrambled eggs and a heated biscuit, sometimes topped with gravy. Along with the breakfast fare came extra strong coffee poured into one's canteen cup. Most of the food items served in our mess tent at lunch and dinner came from the C-ration boxes. The ones I had helped to guard on the beach when we first arrived. In order to make scrambled eggs and biscuits, bags of flour and cartons of eggs must have been brought in from a food source in Da Nang. For the most part, we had to make do with what we had on hand. Also, I seem to recall that officers and enlisted ate in the same tent but at separate tables. I don't recall a sign that designated who set where, but we knew our boundaries.

We were required to wash the trays we used by dipping and scrubbing them in a garbage can filled with soapy water followed by immersion in a can with rinse water. This task prevented diarrhea, most of the time. Now, that I think about it, I don't ever recall seeing an officer in the clean-up line. Well, they say rank has its privileges. I guess privates assigned to mess duty did their sanitizing. Maybe I'm being unfair to my superiors. Perhaps, the officers had their own trash-can line somewhere out of sight. I'm sure they didn't want to dip in enlisted water or be seen performing the mundane chore of cleaning a tray.

Since I've berated and belittled officers, I admit that some of them were liked by lower-ranking troops. Out of an abundance of caution, in a combat area, troops aren't required to salute officers. That's to help prevent the enemy's resident sniper from zeroing-in on leadership. In Vietnam we should have required officers to pay us not to salute. One of the officers in our supply unit, a young first-lieutenant, played catch with me. Somehow he had scrounged baseball mitts and a hard-ball. I don't remember how we managed to wind up playing together, but I fancied myself to be a good fast-ball pitcher. I'd throw the ball at him with all my might and speed. He always caught it without any difficulty. I enjoyed his kindness. I returned it by not saluting him.

I can't recall the lieutenant's name or the names of other Marines in our outfit. I didn't stay in touch with them. I very much regret that. I'd love to talk with them again. The lieutenant hailed from a northern state, and I remember him telling me that back home, he had a Studebaker. That surprised me. I pictured him to be more of a sports car type. I suppose, it may have been a money issue. Another officer, a captain, whenever we stood guard duty on the same night, would talk to me in a casual and relaxed manner. He talked about his college days and made me long for that opportunity. I didn't speak with or have a good relationship with any other officer. Officers aren't supposed to fraternize with enlisted troops in order to maintain a proper chain of command. The time might come when they would need to order you into harm's way, without hesitation. Friendship might impede such an order.

Once fed, Marines sashayed off to work. Okay, Marines don't sashay. Well, there may be a few who did on the weekends back in the states, but that's none of my business. At any rate, we returned to the mess tent for lunch at noontime and later, after work hours, we had dinner at 1700. The evening meal went an hour earlier than usual in order to accommodate Marines assigned to guard duty. The evening watch began at 1800. That's 6:00 p.m. civilian time.

Most work stations, like our living quarters, were housed in general purpose tents. I wrote earlier, that I had been assigned to the Shop Stores tent, issuing small parts to those in need. Later, I moved to another tent and a clerical position. I kept track of our battalion's receipts, amounting to millions of dollars. The Marine who replaced me in Shop

Stores proved to be an enterprising fellow, a true entrepreneur. He had the savvy to hold on to his money until able to travel into nearby Da Nang. He then purchased items for re-sale, cigarettes and so forth. He set up his own general store operation, at marked-up prices. At work, he operated his store along with his Shop Stores duties. Marines who desired such items, helped him to earn a tidy profit. I admired his moxie, but later he earned my dislike when I caught him cheating at cards.

In the evening hours, with our tent drawn closed, we often played cards by candlelight. Being restricted to our camp narrowed the choice of evening entertainment. The Marine who ran his own general store, operated a Black Jack Casino in his tent. Meaning, of course, that he played every game and always dealt the cards. His ability to win hands repeatedly is what first captured my attention. Despite his run of good luck, some Marines continued to play with him. Something about a Marine and his money are soon parted comes to mind. Oh well, back to my Sherlock Holmes moment. I realized that playing under fair odds, he wouldn't be winning so often. I made a point to watch rather than play. It took me a while, longer then I care to admit, but I finally caught on to his method of cheating.

After each hand had been played, he collected the discarded cards and put them face up on the bottom of the deck. That's normal procedure. When he dealt the final card, determining whether his opponent won or lost, his procedure became erratic. He often shouted phrases. The one I remember is "Up jumped the devil!" At the same time, he made a sweeping motion with his hand, slamming the card face-up on the small piece of plywood he used as a card table. With uncanny regularity, his final card beat his opponent's hand, and he collected the greenbacks.

Watching his action, it became clear to me, the sudden movement of his hand and his loud cry were intentional to distract and mask his thievery. When he picked up the cards from the previous hand, he placed a face card or a ten on the bottom of the deck. When he needed a high card to cause his opponent's defeat, he dealt from the bottom of the deck. At first, I didn't notice the bottom-deck dealing. He did a good job of concealing it, but after a while I made a point of memorizing the cards played in the previous hand. That's when I realized his winning card came from the bottom of the deck.

I exposed his cheating trick to others, some of whom demanded their money back in rather harsh terms. Of course, after I outed him, he and I never spoke to one another again. Also, I reported his general store operation, and the staff NCO in charge of our supply unit, made him shut it down. Yeah, go ahead and call me a snitch, but revenge is sweet. Undeterred, the cheating rat moved his general store operation to his sleeping quarters and operated out of his foot locker. He continued to make a profit selling items to those Marines willing to pay high prices due to their lack of deferred gratification and their failure to plan ahead.

After working hours, a make-shift, thatched-roof club on the top of our hill provided cold beer, but it didn't have music or female companionship. Other than that, there wasn't much to do besides playing cards and writing letters home. I didn't have a girl friend back home, so I didn't write many letters. In the evening, when not assigned guard duty, I would rest on my cot and listened to a BBC broadcast of jazz music on my portable radio. That pretty much sums up nightly entertainment options for units like ours camped out in the field.

Taking a stroll outside of our camp by one's self wasn't a good idea. We didn't have permission to do that anyway, but some troopers did take their personal cameras when going out on patrol during daytime. They got some interesting photos, such as Vietnamese children standing on the backs of domesticated water buffalo. The villagers who lived in the nearby hamlets only offered an opportunity for candid photography. They were too busy working to stop and pose for Marines who turned their search and destroy mission to a sight-seeing and photo opt patrol.

From our hilltop, I recall watching a villager scoop water out of the river onto the rice paddies below. He used some sort of basket-looking contraption connected on one end to a pole. From a distance the basket appeared to be made from bamboo. He would swing the basket out onto the river and then swing it back, pouring water he scooped onto the paddy. The rice paddies were sectioned off, but openings could be made to allow water to flow from one paddy to the next when needed. The villager worked at the chore for what seemed like hours at a time without stopping. I wish I had taken a photo of him. Also, the sunrises and sunsets in Vietnam were incredible. And, I suspect that there must have been wild and colorful birds fluttering about, but I don't remember seeing any.

In Vietnam, due to our serious mission, we worked six days a week. We were able to rest on Sunday, unless we were assigned to ambush or guard duty. On the Sabbath, some Marines attended religious services held in the open by a military chaplain. Others, like myself, were devoted to an outdoor Sunday game of Pinochle. We did not play for money; however, cheating still occurred. The game is played with one pair of partners competing against another pair. It's a two-person team sport.

When the cards were dealt, it helped to know the dominant suit your partner held. In secret, partners agreed on signals, so they could communicate their strongest set of cards. Still, the game depended more upon skill than cheating. Signals were, for the most part, neutralized since all players used them. Maybe somewhere in the world there's a Marine who doesn't cheat at cards, but I never met him. I think that's because honest Marines don't tend to play cards.

On Sundays we also played softball on the hilltop. I cheated at that, too. Once when playing second base, with a runner on my base, I called time-out in order to confer with the pitcher. Standing close to him, I asked for the ball. Concealing it in my glove, I returned to second base and after resuming play, under the pretense of wanting to clean the base, I asked the runner to step off the bag. The trusting Marine complied, and, pulling the ball out of my mitt, I made a big show of tagging him out. I know I'm an a-hole, and, though it may not matter now, I regret that I did that. The Marine may hate me for humiliating him in the name of sport. Well, most people are flawed in some way, or that's just a flimsy excuse I use to justify my poor behavior.

I almost forgot. At night, if not on guard duty, we could go to our outdoor movie. A movie screen had been made by painting plywood panels white and scattering sand on the wet paint. Seats were squared-off logs arranged on the ground. I never did know, or care to ask, where the logs came from. However, I remember one night, while watching a film, hearing a big commotion coming from nearby.

To our west, an ARVN boot camp conducted night-time training, and their sound carried in the night's stillness. A few miles to the north of our campsite, beyond the artillery unit, loomed Hill 327, site of 9th Marines HQ. That's were planning and strategy for Marine operations played out. To our south, lie the expanse of Happy Valley, where fighting often occurred far into evening hours, sometimes throughout the night. Talking about being surreal, with the loud night-practice by ARVN recruits a hill or two over; planning of hostile engagements by senior Marine officers at HQ to the north of us; and actual fighting by armed troops within earshot to the south; we sat watching film of a television series, *Combat.*

In the days ahead, the plywood movie screen took three live rounds during an infantry attack. In memory of the event, the holes were never repaired. After that, Marines attended fewer night movies. Due to work requirements, we didn't have daytime showings, but I liked to call the cautious Marines, "Matinee Marines." Being one of the braver types, I continued to attend the late evening movies on a regular basis, but no longer without my helmet, flak jacket, and rifle.

The films we watched came from Special Services at the Da Nang Air Base. Marines selected to make the run in order to acquire more films and return the ones we had watched, also brought back beer and ice for our enlisted club. The club had been constructed by our own troops out of bamboo and palm fronds. The palm fronds were used for the roof. The make-shift structure stood on the very apex of the hill, not the safest of locations for a club. Still, if you're going to be shot at, might as well have a beer in your hand. Sometimes it's all about logistics. The hilltop provided the only available space for the club's location. Better a club exposed on the hill than no club at all.

One day several of us were allowed to leave work to accompany the company armorer, a staff sergeant, to the foot of an unoccupied hill near Hill 327. There the armorer set-up a target at the base of the hill and positioned an M-60 machine gun a few hundred yards out in front. We were allowed to fire the gun for familiarization. When my turn came, I took my time and fired a couple of single shots. The sergeant, criticized me for not firing in full-automatic mode. I explained that I was just sighting-in and fired off another single shot and adjusted the gun sight. Then, before he could complain any more, I held back on the gun's trigger and riddled the target dead center. Looking somewhat surprised, the sergeant complimented me on my good shooting. Not that it mattered, but I felt redeemed from his earlier criticism.

We had visitors on a few occasions that interrupted the day's routine. We were once inspected by Lieutenant General Victor H. "Brute" Krulak, Commanding General, Fleet Marine Force, Pacific, headquartered in Hawaii. We had been advised before the inspection to keep our eyes straight ahead and not look down at the general. Krulak stood only 5 feet, 4 inches tall, hence his nickname, given when he attended the Naval Academy. I did notice that he wore a .45-caliber, pearl-handled, sidearm. I suspect, only generals can get away with changing plain pistol grips to pearl-handled. And, in my humble opinion, only ego-eccentric generals would want to. I understand, Army General, George S. Patton, not known for subtlety, sometimes wore two.

Krulak's exemplary military career made up for his lack of height and ego issues. Some military historians believe that he would have been selected Commandant of the Marine Corps, had he not butted heads with Army General Westmoreland over military strategy employed in South Vietnam. President Lyndon Johnson sided with Westmoreland and passed over Krulak for the Marine Corps's top position. Westmoreland prevailed and promptly set about losing the war, thinking that superior fire power and advanced technology would carry the day. He never realized that the fighting hinged, according to

Pulitzer-prize winning author, David Halberstam, on North Vietnam's birthrate. North Vietnam would keep sending troops as long as they had them to send. Bottom-line, kill some and more would follow. And, Westmoreland did little to win the support of the South Vietnamese people, part of the strategy proposed by General Krulak. Later, LBJ, realizing he had approved a failing strategy and lost the confidence of the American public, chose not to run for re-election.

One bright, sunny day, the professional golfer, Billy Casper, paid an unexpected visit to our camp. Casper had 51 PGA tournament wins, seventh on the all-time list. Most of his wins came in the 1950s and '60s; however, he did win the prestigious Masters tournament in 1970. He didn't have the long drive of Palmer or Nicklaus, but he won tournaments with his accuracy.

A few other Marines and I were allowed to accompany him up to the top of our hill where he drove some golf balls into the rice paddies below. He also aimed at the Vietnamese farmers and their water buffalo, while they were plowing the paddies. He came close, but didn't hit them, so I thought maybe he didn't really intend to. At least, that's what I chose to believe. He seemed like a nice guy, but so do some assassins.

Once, while standing outside my work tent, taking a break from recording the million and one invoices that flowed through our battalion, I spied a tank coming into our camp at a high rate of speed, kicking up a trail of dust. Sitting on top of the tank's gun turret, rode a civilian dressed in a plaid, felt shirt and khaki pants tucked into a pair of high-topped boots.

Stupid, correspondent, I thought to myself.

I had nothing against correspondents, except I didn't appreciate the show-boating. It seemed to trivialize the war and our participation in it. When the tank drew closer, I recognized its rider, none other than Charlton Heston, the famous movie actor. Even from my distant vantage point, he looked bigger than life. I forgave him for show-boating. After all, I suppose that's normal routine, if you're a famous movie star.

Word came down from the company office that troops could be dismissed in order to meet Mr. Heston at our hill-top club house. One Marine had to stay behind in each work tent, until the others returned. I didn't volunteer, but I got picked anyway. I regretted not being able to meet the actor. I had seen many of his movies, including lesser known ones, such as one of my favorites, *The Naked Jungle*. I saw that movie just days before enlisting in the Marine Corps.

After several minutes had passed, I went to the back opening of the work tent to have a smoke and wallow in my pity party. As luck would have it, sometimes out of misfortune opportunity presents itself. Heston and a few staff Marines, having finished meeting the troops at our clubhouse, came walking by the backside of my work tent headed to the Amtrack Unit behind us, I suppose to do another "meet and greet." Tank battalion troops, in no hurry to return to work, remained at the club to quaff another brew or two. The actor walked by me for ten feet or so. I regretted not speaking out to him, but, to my surprise, he turned and came back to me and stuck out his hand.

Like a giddy school boy, I shook his hand and said, "Mr. Heston, I certainly have enjoyed your movies."

He replied, "Corporal, I appreciate that."

Heston had a firm grip and impressed me with his height and broad chest. I knew that some actors didn't measure up to their movie presence when in public. One of my favorites, Alan Ladd, of "Shane" fame, stood on a box whenever filmed close-up with a taller actor. At least, that's what I read.

I'll always remember Heston's smile, it seemed natural and sincere, not forced. He seemed to me to be a big man with a gentle soul. Then off he went, like a ship passing in the night, with the staff sergeants trailing behind. Later in life, Heston's politics differed from mine. Yet, I regretted that he suffered dementia before his death. I will always appreciate his kind words and gesture.

Once I managed to a attend a showing just outside of Da Nang featuring the comedian and movie star, Bob Hope. I seem to remember that Ann Margaret accompanied him, but I'm not certain. Over the years, pleasurable experiences have eroded from my mind more than anything else. It's easier to remember the bad. Negative experiences have a way of sticking with you. At any rate, Hope always included a good-looking female star in his routines, and this performance held true to form, no pun intended. I recall everyone in the crowd laughed at his jokes. I don't remember any of them, but I do remember him referring to Da Nang as a "mud depot." At the time, it seemed like a strange remark given that the monsoon season had not yet arrived and our roads were still dusty.

I read that Johnny Carson disliked Hope and regretted having him guest star on his late-night television program. Carson complained that Hope insisted on staying "on script" and refused to engage in off-the-cuff conversation. Perhaps, the comedian had scripted his remark about Da Nang being muddy, and, when arriving during the country's dry season, failed to remember to alter his script. At least, after reading Carson's remarks, that's my take on it.

At night, when not playing cards, I reclined on my cot with my Sony 9 transistor radio sitting on my chest. I purchased the radio in

Okinawa at our base's PX and carried it with me to South Vietnam.

The radio had a black shiny case that looked lacquered and had silver-colored trim. Years later, while watching the movie, *Good morning, Vietnam*, I noticed in one scene, a trooper on a transport truck carrying the same identical radio. At any rate, with it close to my head, I played it with the volume turned down low, since I didn't have earphones and didn't want to disturb anyone.

My radio had short-wave capability, so I listened to a BBC broadcast of jazz music. When a teenager, I only listened to Rock & Roll. The AFRTS station, operating out of Saigon, did play rock hits, but, to the best of my memory, only in the daytime. We didn't play a radio at work very often, so I listened to night-time broadcasts. Now, having turned 21, I found myself listening to the likes of the Red Norvo Octet, with Norvo playing such hits as "Blues in E Flat" on the vibraphone. On an occasion or two, I listened to classical music, but I preferred jazz. Some people claim maturity is accelerated by adversity.

It's trivial, but I think I should mention that our haircuts were provided by a fellow Marine. He volunteered for the job. He had a comb and scissors, so that qualified him. Long lines formed whenever he set up his operation. Somehow he managed to keep our hair cut close. Despite his availability, my hair often exceeded regulations. I hated standing in line and would avoid it until I couldn't anymore.

Since we were either tromping through dust or mud, we weren't required to keep our boots shined. A privilege in the Marine Corps only found in a war zone. Besides, my shoe polish, Kiwi in a can, if left opened for even a single day, dried to a bone-like consistency. We also didn't shine our brass buckles or tips of our web belts, an act of negligence that would have gotten us recommended for court martial back in the states. I exaggerate but not by much.

Vietnamese providing laundry service, were assigned a pick-up and delivery site at the back edge of our camp just outside my work tent. I do get lucky from time to time. They returned the dirty clothes within two or three days. The washed and ironed items would be wrapped in cellophane. From time to time, I would rinse an article or two of clothing that didn't seem clean enough in my helmet, and place it on the edge of the tent to dry in the sun.

Well, I think that about summarizes our daily routine.

Dangerous incidents were infrequent. Most were those you heard about, ones that happened to someone in another unit. Unless you count the occasional rounds fired by a Viet Cong sniper. None of us wanted to harm him, due to his inability to hit his intended target. We feared his replacement might be a better shot. Of course, the sniper's desire for concealment and to avoid capture or death, meant firing from a bamboo thicket five or six hundred yards across the rice paddies.

Still, reports of even a few violent incidents were too frequent for an anti-hero like me. Unlike most others, I remained weary of the sniper due to my strong desire to survive. I think the sniper and I shared that in common. He stayed hidden on the other side of the rice paddy to the south of our camp, and I tried to remain unseen to him. Who knows, maybe today we'd be friends. Like myself, he didn't actually shoot anyone, although he tried often enough. Yet, I hold no grudge against him. He just followed orders and fought for his homeland.

Chapter 6

Guard Duty

Linking up with the Ontos unit on our west flank, our camp's defensive perimeter wrapped around the front, south side of Hill 34. After 75 yards or so, it extended back along our east flank until hooking up with the AmTrack unit to the north of our camp. We had multiple work units on the hill, including supply platoon. In addition to their occupational duties, each had guard-duty responsibility for a designated portion of the perimeter.

I don't know why our platoon got picked to guard the hill's south side, overlooking Happy Valley. Maybe we were selected after straws were drawn. I never attended a command briefing, so some details weren't shared with me. For all I know, our officers made decisions by flipping a coin or using a Ouija board. Nah, they're military. They need to inflict pain. I'm sure they threw steel-tipped darts at a cardboard target labeled, "Yes, No, Maybe."

To the southwest corner of our camp, near the Ontos section, we had a bunker housing a heavy .50-caliber machine-gun mounted on a large tripod. The .50-caliber, with a weight of 84 lbs., is so powerful that it has wooden handles that you gripped while pressing its butterfly shaped trigger with your thumbs. Its rate of fire, 450 rounds per minute, is slow when compared to the rapid fire of smaller automatic weapons. However, the size of its rounds, 5.45 inches in length, and their destructive power more than compensated for its slowness.

I heard that the Geneva Convention prohibited the .50-caliber machine gun from being used on enemy troops. The .50-caliber only had approval for use against motorized vehicles and for anti-aircraft defense. Despite such restrictions, we placed the large weapon in one of our bunkers, the one we called the "right 50," facing the southern, right flank corner. We had arrived in a war zone without enough of the newer M60 machine guns, so we used what we had. We felt that our survival depended upon it.

To the left of the "right 50," we positioned a bunker midway our area of responsibility. We designated the bunker as the "center 30," due to its location and being outfitted with a .30-caliber machine-gun. The old .30-caliber, Browning M1919 saw action in WWII and Korea. When first produced, the gun had a water-cooled barrel. At least, we had the newer air-cooled version. Still, it should have been replaced, but, again, in desperate times you use what you have.

Back behind the "center 30," a "command post" bunker stood atop the crest of the hill. From there, an officer and a staff NCO took turns watching over us to insure we stayed alert. I suppose they thought their bravery could be proven by having the CP bunker in an exposed position. Of course, they could also get a better view of the countryside and the Vietnamese women bathing in the river below. Honest, I never noticed that activity, but others told me about it.

To the left of the "center 30" we had a bunker designated as the "left 60" since it housed an M60 machine-gun mounted on a bi-pod. All of our machine-guns were belt-fed. To protect ammo from the elements, the belt-connected ammo came housed in metal canisters. You had only to open the lid on the canister and feed one end of the belt into the gun's receiver. When ready to fire, you pulled back on the gun's bolt, and then let it go forward, thus injecting a round into the chamber. Then you had only to aim, and pull the trigger back, and hold it. Rounds would come out in streams. The rapid-fire guns would eject the ammo casings like a redneck spitting out watermelon seeds, only a heck of a lot faster.

The M60 fired 750 rounds per minute. If you haven't done the math, that's 12.5 rounds per second. In the bunker, it sat on a bi-pod mounted to its barrel. The bi-pod could be folded back along the sides of the barrel, and, due to its light weight, the weapon could be fired from the hip. Although to do so required strong muscles and steady nerves. The M60 fired the same 7.62 mm round used in our even lighter, semi-automatic M-14 rifles, although much faster.

Having said that, I must add that the company armorer, as a favor to me, altered my M-14 by filing the rifle's sear and installing a selector-switch. By turning the switch, I could convert my weapon from semi-automatic to full-automatic. Of course, if I did so, the M-14 's magazine, holding only 20 rounds of 7.62 mm ammo, would be emptied in a matter of seconds. We carried four magazines on our cartridge belt, so firing in automatic mode meant you'd soon be left with only an empty rifle and a bayonet for protection. Firing the M-14 in full-on automatic would be foolish except in a dire situation.

In summary, supply company manned a "right 50" bunker, a "center 30" bunker, a "left 60" bunker, and a "CP" bunker. I seem to remember, the bunkers, not including the "command post," were about 20-30 yards apart and were connected by trenches. When signaled by the banging on an artillery shell hanging from a chain, our fellow Marines, who had been resting in the tent area, would don their combat equipment, grab their rifles, and would rush to their assigned positions in our perimeter trenches.

The bunkers housing machine guns on the hill's south side had been positioned below the crest of the hill. That way they did not present a silhouetted target to the enemy. On the down side, troops rallying to fill in the trenches between those bunkers had to go over the hill's crest. They needed to be quick about it. Doing so exposed them to possible enemy fire. If firing had already commenced, the safest thing for them to do would be to crawl over.

Officers and staff-sergeants who manned the "command post" bunker, only carried a side-arm, a .45-caliber Colt 1911A1 semi-automatic pistol. Since pistols wouldn't have been effective if waves of

Viet Cong were charging up our hill, I assumed the officers and staff-sergeants carried pistols in order to shoot any enlisted Marine who might decide to desert his post. I'm just kidding. Everybody knows officers would be the first to run. Not really, we were all brave Marines. None of us gave serious thought to running. The bunkers and trenches were far safer than being exposed in open terrain.

Years earlier, French forces had defended Hill 34 in their failed war effort. The hill did not appear to have been well fortified by them. Evidence of a weak defense could be seen in a few one-man foxholes, about two and a half feet in diameter, scattered across the hill's ridge. We filled those in with gravel and used them for urinals. In fair turnabout, I imagine our bunkers have now been converted into outhouses or septic tanks. It would be a fitting end to a lost cause. I'm certain most Vietnamese would agree.

Our sand-bagged bunkers were about 8 foot square. The front of each bunker extended beyond its three-foot deep hole, so that the machine-gun had an earthen shelf to sit on. And, to the rear of the bunker we placed a cot for resting. In addition to the machine-gun, there were other defensive armaments in the bunkers. To one side of the machine-gun set canisters of belt ammo, a detonator for a Claymore mine, and a few grenades. The M61 fragmentation grenades were known as "lemon" grenades due to their shape. They replaced the MK-II grenades from WWII. Those grenades had vertical and horizontal grooves on their cast-iron body and were known as "pineapple" grenades. Also, along with the canisters of ammo and the grenades, we were equipped with an M-79 single-shot, shoulder-fired grenade launcher. The weapon looked like a stubby, sawed-off shot-gun with a wide, round barrel that earned the nickname, "Can Cannon." The weapon fired a 40mm explosive round for up to 430 yards.

Claymore mines had been positioned about 20 feet out in front of each bunker, just behind barbed-wire fencing that enclosed our hill. The M18A1 Claymore mine, rectangular in shape, stood only 4.9 inches tall by 8.5 inches in length and only 1.5 inches in width. "Front Toward Enemy" had been stamped on one side to prevent Marines from aiming the mine at themselves. Fired by remote control from inside the bunker, it shot a wide pattern of metal balls, like a shot-gun without a choke, for up to 55 yards.

The barbed-wire fencing had been strung with tin cans attached that contained a few small rocks to serve as a primitive early-warning system. In addition, trip-flares were strung out in front of the barbed wire. Grass and weeds growing in the fencing were burned from time to time using a hand-held torch device. When I performed the burning duty, I liked to entertain villagers by waving flames up into the air. They would stop whatever they were doing to watch. It seemed that Vietnamese were fascinated by fire. On occasion, our company commander would order a M67 Zippo Tank to shoot a stream of fire, known as "rod of flame," from our hilltop into the night's sky to let any Viet Cong in the area know that we had incinerating capability.

From our camp, every evening a villager could be heard striking, what sounded to me like a section of a large, hollowed bamboo. The first three or four taps were slow and spaced at even intervals and then the tapping increased to a rapid rate before trailing off to silence. I didn't know the purpose of the ritual, but I assumed the Vietnamese prayed at the end of the work day and maybe tapped on bamboo to get Buddha's attention. I'm a spiritual, not a religious person, but when I stood guard duty every third night and heard that tapping sound, I hoped the Vietnamese were praying for peace. I though God, if there is one, would answer their prayers before mine. Well, I never prayed. Perhaps I should have.

Guard duty on a moonlit night had advantages. For one, any movement could be seen and reacted to in quick fashion. Thus, the moonlight helped to ensure a quiet, peaceful night with no need for firing illumination flares. The lunar glow also reflected off the water in the rice paddies, creating an artistic appearance, like a Monet landscape painting. On such nights, I liked to sit on the top of a bunker to be able to better see the moon and stars and the beauty of the countryside. I could almost forget about the war and just revel in the scenery. I even liked to sleep on top of a bunker under my poncho when it rained. I found the the patter of the raindrops to be soothing.

One early evening, with the sun still overhead, I climbed on top of a bunker to take in the daytime view. Within a couple of minutes, I felt the air part next to the right side of my face followed by a *twing* sound. Damn, I had no doubt about it. I had been shot at by a sniper and almost hit. Sitting there upright, I had made myself a convenient and inviting target. Because of the position in which I had been facing when I felt the gush of air, I knew the shot had come from the bamboo thicket across the rice paddies to the southwest of me. I never told anyone about the incident. I didn't see the need. We all knew that the danger of sniper fire existed in our area. Besides, I never saw another Marine sitting on top of a bunker in broad daylight. They either had better sense than yours truly, or they lacked appreciation for the scenery. I prefer to think the latter.

Wanting to display a calm demeanor and coolness of character, I faced the direction in which the shot had been fired and gave the sniper a wave of my hand, my way of saying, "Hi there." Then, without further hesitation, I climbed down to safety. I had no intention of waiting for him to adjust his sights and provide him with a second opportunity. I wondered how he reacted to my waving at him. I hoped that it made him see my human side, rather than my being just a static target. Then again, he may not have cared or noticed. Like the Ontos, he may have felt it best to shoot and scoot.

We didn't have a Marine sniper in our outfit. In fact, we were under orders not to fire at anyone without first getting our company commander (CO) to verify the danger. Even at night, when villagers were required to be in their hamlets, if we saw movement we couldn't fire. We had to send someone to wake-up the CO and wait for him come and inspect the situation. In short, we were not allowed to fire first. It reminded me of the old country adage, "Never throw the first blow, but give the second one all you've got."

Rules of engagement in South Vietnam, put us at a disadvantage. I decided that if a person or persons advanced on our camp in the dark, I might not wait for someone to fetch the CO. If I called out and the unidentified person or persons failed to identify themselves and continued to advance, a Claymore mine might somehow be detonated by accident. I'm sure clumsier things have happened. If need be, I'd apologize to the CO. Besides, what could he do to me worse than my getting killed due to a stupid requirement?

After being shot at, I did my daylight viewing using binoculars from either the camp's perimeter trench or from inside a bunker. In truth, I don't remember climbing on top of a bunker ever again. Well, maybe I did on dark, moonless nights. There were times when I wanted to stay outside the confines of the small, two-man bunkers. During the night, swarms of mosquitoes would invade the bunkers. The were quite annoying. After complaining for a few weeks, we were provided with small, plastic bottles of repellent that proved effective. I suppose we got the repellent because officers were also being bitten.

Standing guard throughout the evening and early morning hours could be eerie on those nights with no moon. You had the feeling that Viet Cong could be maneuvering towards you, unseen in the dark. The tank crews, equipped with a 26.5mm flare gun that looked like a fat, stubby pistol, would help illuminate the situation. They fired parachute flares at varied intervals throughout the darkest nights, aiming them out over the rice paddies. The flares drifted back to earth in about a minute or so, but during their descent each one would light up about 15 acres. Also, situated above a tank's main gun, a one million candle power, Xenon searchlight had the capability of turning dark to day; however, the intense light made an inviting target, so they weren't often used.

Moonlight helped eliminate paranoia. Without the lunar illumination, we welcomed the firing of parachute flares. However, every time a flare ignited in the sky, roosters in the nearby hamlets would commence crowing. It never failed. You could hear them becoming frazzled as the night wore on. With flares being shot off throughout the night, the roosters failed to crow at daybreak. Having somewhat of a rural background, I felt sorry for them and their hoarse throats. The roosters were an early casualty of the war. Still, it provided a sense of relief to be able to see into the night and realize the encroaching enemy to be just a figment of one's imagination. To paraphrase Franklin D. Roosevelt, president during an earlier war, "We had nothing to fear but . . . fear of the dark."

Chapter 7

Liberty Call

A few times during my stay in Vietnam, five or six other Marines and I, each of us from different work units, got to leave camp at noon and head into Da Nang for a few hours of liberty. Liberty call is when you're allowed to leave the base camp and go out on your own in search of a good time. Since we were not acquainted with each other, we went our separate ways. I welcomed the free time, but nothing good lasts forever. Sometimes it's over sooner than you anticipated. We had to meet back by 1800 at a prearranged area to re-board the transport truck for the return trip to Hill 34.

The first time I went on liberty in Vietnam, I had almost six hours to explore Da Nang and enjoy a well-earned taste of freedom. Speaking of taste, first order of business for me would be obtaining a good civilian-style meal. I wanted one that had not been dumped out of a C-ration box. I didn't know the location of any good restaurants. I just kept looking until I found one that appealed to me.

The search would have been easier if I had not been distracted by a dozen or more young boys tagging along, badgering me for money. I don't remember any girls among them. Despite their constant begging, the young lads did not appear to be famished or impoverished. At any rate, I kept telling them, "No money, no money." Kids know when they're lied to, so they persisted.

When I neared the inner-city area, the young boys gave up and wandered off. Along the way, I noticed what I believed to be homes of the well-to-do. The houses were walled-in like fortresses. Their walls, about seven feet high, had jagged glass mortared onto their tops. I doubted that they were intended to keep out begging kids. I suspected something more sinister. It made me wonder if anywhere in South Vietnam offered safe haven. Still, I must say that the Vietnamese people I observed displayed a casual demeanor. I suppose, war or no war, life goes on.

The restaurant I selected, situated along a street that ran parallel with the Da Nang River, had outdoor seating under shade trees. It made for a pleasant site, with a peaceful view of the river, remote from the hardships of war. I remember that I ordered a steak. I'm not sure what I had with it, but I do recall that the meat had an agreeable flavor but seemed a bit chewy. I wondered if I had been served low-grade beef or an old water buffalo, no longer fit to plow rice paddies. I dismissed my cynicism and tried to enjoy the meal in the restaurant's calm setting. Before long, a young boy interrupted my meal. Unlike the beggars that nagged me earlier, he wore a smile and carried a shoe shine box.

"Hey, mister. You want me to shine your boots? Only 90 piastres."

Well, maybe it wasn't 90. It's been a long time. I do remember that, by my calculation, he asked for the equivalent of .50 cents, which seemed reasonable to me. Still, I knew that having my boots shined, given living conditions on Hill 34, amounted to a waste of money. However, this boy wanted to earn money, not beg for it. After my earlier pestering, I appreciated that and decided to reward him by agreeing to his request.

I had a panoramic view of the river to my right. To my left, and at a lower level, a young French couple with two small children were seated. Adjacent to them, set three older Frenchmen, all seemed a bit over-weight. France still maintained an embassy in Da Nang. I suspected they were all, in some way, associated with it. The young couple and their children were soft spoken. In contrast, the three men conversed in louder voices. I could hear them far better than I wanted to. They spoke French in a rapid rate that exceeded my ability to understand what they said. However, by the tone of their conversation, I detected negativity. I felt my presence may not have been welcomed.

Unable to contain himself any longer, one of the three older types blurted out his disapproval in English, "That's too much. Before you Americans came, we never paid them more than a nickel."

I looked directly at him, shrugged my shoulders just a little, and, mustering up my best high school French, replied, "*Ca ne fait rien.*"

In English, that translates to: "It doesn't matter, never mind."

I didn't know many French phrases, but the one I did remember seemed quite appropriate. Years later I had the opportunity to repeat the phrase to a French-speaking Canadian. She said she understood me, and offered the exact same translation. I felt relieved to know that I had, without a doubt, been understood at the restaurant in Da Nang. Even back then, I had reason to believe that my French did not fail me. For the remainder of the time I spent at the restaurant, the Frenchmen did not utter another word. You could have heard a napkin hit the floor.

I had delivered the phrase with correct pronunciation and topped it off with casual body language. I believe that they thought that I had understood everything they had said and were mortified. At least, that's the way it came across to me. What I do know for certain is that, while we may have lost the war in Vietnam, on that day I trounced an arrogant Frenchman.

Having finished my meal, and with my boots shined, I decided to get a professional haircut. I had nothing against our camp's volunteer barber, but every time I sought him out, he had a line of Marines waiting their turn. Waiting had never been my strong suit, so I walked around Da Nang looking for a barbershop. I searched for a barber's pole, hoping Vietnamese used the same signage as we did back in America.

Instead, I found a middle-aged, Vietnamese male. He had a chair and folding table replete with tonic, towel, comb, scissors, and a thin-bladed knife but no barber's pole. He had his outdoor barbershop set up by a sidewalk in the downtown area. I hadn't had my hair cut in a month, and I risked getting into trouble if I put it off any longer. By Marine Corps standards, I needed a trim three weeks ago, so I decided to give the Vietnamese barber a try. It appealed to me that he had no other customers, no waiting line.

Besides the fact that he cut hair outdoors beside a sidewalk, I recall how, along with the haircut, he massaged my forehead, just above my nose. He employed a sort of pinching action. It may not have been intentional, but it caused me to pass out for a brief moment. I almost fell out of the chair. In fact, I would have, had he not caught me. I supposed I had been stressed out and just didn't realize it. At any rate, the barber said something to another Vietnamese male standing nearby, and the two of them laughed. Since I had been rescued from an abrupt fall, I didn't have a problem with being laughed at. One matter that did concern me had to do with the barber's dislike for stray hair. He trimmed a hair growing somewhere on the inner surface of one of my ears. He used what looked like an old, kitchen knife with a sharp, narrow blade.

It occurred to me that he could have finished my existence on earth by plunging the knife deep into my ear canal. I guess Viet Cong are too busy infiltrating and fighting to bother cutting hair in a downtown setting. Even if the barber had been a VC sympathizer, he must have felt the time not right to reveal his allegiance. Maybe, he had no political preference and just wanted to earn a living. At any rate, whatever the case, I felt a sense of relief when he placed the knife back on the small, folding table.

After the badgering by kids, the rudeness of the Frenchman, the experience of a brief black out, and concern about the narrow blade, I decided to ease my tension with a frothy brew. I looked for a small bar with few customers. I just wanted to relax without a lot of hullabaloo. On a side street I found a bar with only one other customer. I went in and ordered a beer. I remember it being labeled "33 Beer." I have since learned that it had been brewed from rice. The beer tasted okay, not the best I've ever had, but it satisfied me.

I sipped on my beer, minding my own business. At last, I had begun to feel at ease. Then the other customer ruined my peaceful moment. An ARVN soldier in uniform, he spoke up and said, "We don't want your air-conditioners." He surprised me by speaking in perfect English and confused me with his comment.

"I'm sorry. I don't understand," I replied.

"You Americans want to make Vietnam like U.S.A., big cars and air-conditioners."

He acted agitated, so I finished the last sip of my beer. I didn't want any trouble, so without saying another word, I got up and walked out. I gave up on my afternoon of liberty, deciding it to be a hopeless pursuit. It seemed to me that I would be better off alone. I returned to the designated pick-up area. With the other Marines no where in sight, I propped against a tree, lit a cigarette, and waited for the return of the transport truck. I would go on liberty a few more times while in South Vietnam and have better experiences. However, on that day, I agreed with John Milton's quote from *Paradise Lost*, "Solitude is sometimes best society."

Chapter 8

Patrol/Ambush

While in South Vietnam, I participated in two different types of patrols, company and squad. I first went out on a company patrol. Later, after being promoted to corporal, I led squad patrols of the neighboring hamlets. The company patrol I remember consisted of Marines drawn from various platoons of H & S Company. During morning hours, we assembled at the top of Hill 34 and were informed we would be doing a "search and sweep" patrol. The patrol would cross the rice paddies directly to the south of our base camp and sweep through the hamlet hidden from sight by bamboo thickets, palm trees, and other vegetation.

As best as I can remember, there were about 15 or 20 of us in the company patrol. Since we worked in different units, I knew some of them but not all. Still, we were all Marines. We had the same combat training and knew how to work as a team. Leaving our camp in daylight, we made no attempt to conceal our action. So, I decided we were, in reality, just making a show of our presence to any VC that might be lurking in the area. We crossed the rice paddies in single file, too close to each other to suit me. We had been trained in boot camp not to bunch up for fear that one grenade would kill several Marines, or that machine-gun fire could easily mow down a tight column.

At any rate, I considered the point man to be in the most danger, having to look for land-mines and booby-traps on the ground while scanning for enemy positions at eye level. I preferred, in a company patrol, to position myself somewhere near the middle of the column. I reasoned that mines would take out those in the front of the column and sneak attacks would wipe out the rear. I may not have been brave, but I tried to be cautious. You can't fight if you're dead or, even more important to me, live to return home.

After crossing the rice paddy, we reached and entered the bamboo thicket. It surprised me how well the bamboo growth hid the hamlet from view. From Hill 34, I couldn't see the homes of villagers living five or six hundred yards in front of us, but there they were, three or four families with a thatched hut for each. I remember that they had chickens and a haystack. I suppose they kept hay for the water buffalo they used to plow the rice paddies. They didn't seem bothered by our presence, or perhaps they just wanted to avoid confrontation.

Speaking of the haystack, it puzzled me somewhat that the staff sergeant in charge of the patrol did not have it examined. I had seen an article in a news magazine about Viet Cong hiding places. The article included a diagram of a haystack with hollowed center. I though about bringing the matter up, but from somewhere nearby, three or four rifle shots rang out. I guess that the staff sergeant, like the villagers, desired to avoid confrontation. Without delay, he led us back to camp in a hurry.

Once back on the hill, we were dismissed. We returned to work just like any other day. There had been no debriefing, no explanation for our hasty return. Back at work, with a stack of invoices to process, I quit thinking about it. I had too much paperwork to complete. Besides, we were trained to carry out orders and keep our questions, advice, and opinions to ourselves.

After my promotion to corporal, I participated in patrols of the nearby hamlets as squad leader with four other riflemen under my charge. We were assigned to patrol the hamlet to the east side of our camp and the strip of bamboo thicket to the south of our hill at its bottom. The bamboo growth close to the Amtrac Unit served as our debarkation point. Once we slipped into the cover of the bamboo thicket, we headed toward the local hamlet where the bamboo thinned out. With the area more open, rather than proceed in single file, I had my squad fan out. That made for a better sweep of the area. It also made it less likely that we would all be shot at the same time. I led the way despite my proclivity to hang back. My recent promotion forced me into a low-level leadership role.

One of my squad members, after about twenty minutes into the patrol, asked if he could have a drink of my water. He carried two canteens on his cartridge belt, but they were both empty. I kept my irritation to myself and gave him a drink. Later we came to a clearing were, off to one side, stood a picnic-like table with attached seating. The structure had a roof of palm frowns over it. Lying on its table appeared to be an abandoned suitcase. The same Marine who came on patrol without water, started over to the table to inspect it. I should have let the dumb ass do it, but I told him to stop and leave it alone. To me, the suitcase had *booby-trap* written all over it. I ordered the squad to move on.

Villagers did not appear alarmed when we appeared. They greeted us with smiles, most of them with teeth stained dark red from chewing betel nut. The chew provided hard-working Vietnamese with a mild euphoria, something to ease the stress of rural work. Most hamlets in our area had three or more families. Their huts were primitive. They lived as they had for hundreds of years. They seemed to want nothing more than to grow rice and live in peace.

I suspect they greeted VC and U.S. troops in the same manner. They just wanted to be left alone and tend their fields. If the communists won the war, they would have to give up a portion of their rice crop, and if the ARVN and the Americans won out, they would have to pay taxes. They were screwed either way, and they knew it. At least, to me, that seem to be their reaction. I suspect, they paid allegiance to whomever happened to be present in their village. That way they could continue to work and survive.

Our sweeps of local villages were intended to help ensure that Viet Cong troops did not take up residence in the hamlets. During my time spent in Vietnam, our patrols never met resistance. The only unusual occurrence came when I spotted a young girl on a trail. We saw each other at the same time, and she turned and started running away. Because of her reaction, I wondered if she might be a VC scout. I gave chase, shouting, "*Dung lai, dung lai*," meaning "stop." I don't remember how I knew the words, but I did. In fact, it's the only thing I know how to say in Vietnamese.

Somehow, despite the added weight of my rifle, ammo, flak jacket, and other gear, I managed to catch up with her. I never gave thought to shooting her. I preferred she escape rather than cause her injury. Besides, what information could she pass on? We wanted the VC to know we patrolled the area. The young girl posed no real threat. Having said that, when I ran towards her, I looked at her hands to make sure they were empty. I did not want to be recipient of a grenade.

Villagers also came running. I guess they heard my repeated yelling of "Stop!" One Vietnamese male who appeared wore western-style clothes. He had on dark trousers and a white, long-sleeved shirt. The man, maybe 30 years of age, did not have betel nut stained teeth like the villagers. And, he spoke very good English. He explained that the girl came from a nearby village and ran because I scared her. I asked him to tell her that she scared me too. I believe my response helped ease the tension. In truth, I wondered more about the man than the girl, but, like the suit case I spotted, I decided to leave well enough alone.

Besides guard duty and patrols, I stood "river watch" or what we also called, "night ambush." The river that I believed to be the Da Nang river, called *Han* by the Vietnamese, flowed within sight of Hill 34. We kept watch on the river every night in order to prevent VC from floating mortars or other munitions within striking distance of the Da Nang Air Base.

We called it an ambush, but I suspect the enemy knew we were there. Each evening, while still daylight, a squad of Marines would cross the rice paddies and reach the bamboo thicket bordering the river. There we had five single-man, foxholes dug about ten feet apart. We were required to stay awake and monitor the river throughout the entire night.

The river ambush proved to be an uneventful. I had no disappointment with that. I didn't want to shoot anyone. Of course, if the situation had demanded it, I would not have hesitated. I didn't want to die for my country. If anybody had to die, I'd rather it be the enemy. Further, if we encountered a force larger than our squad, we would have had to negotiate our way back through rice paddies in order to reach the safety of our camp. That would mean being exposed in the open. If we were pinned down, we would be trapped in water and mud before reinforcements arrived or the enemy retreated. It would not be a pleasant way to spend the night.

Our ambush strategy concerned me even more. We were all assigned to face the river and look for anything suspicious floating in the water. In the dark it made sense to have more than one set of eyes glued to the river, but I felt uneasy about what might occur behind us. Viet Cong had been known to sneak up from the rear. I developed a sore neck from the frequent turning of my head throughout the night, looking to the rear. Had I been in charge, I would have instructed a couple of Marines to keep watch behind us. In life or death situations, you have to find ways to countermand poor leadership, even it means developing a sore neck.

Chapter 9

R & R

Most of us who served in South Vietnam were given R & R, five consecutive days of free time to unwind from physical and mental stress. Instead of rest and recuperation, some troopers called it rock & roll. Others, unrefined types, preferred I & I for intoxication and intercourse. The five-day vacation included travel time to and from the destination. In reality, it amounted to only three days of relaxation. Marines qualify for R & R only once during their typical 13-month, overseas tour of duty. I've read that Bangkok, Hong Kong, and Tokyo were favorite choices for those fortunate enough to make a choice.

Unlike GIs in other branches of military service, being a low-ranked Marine, I did not have that privilege. While I didn't get to pick my destination, with help from a friend who worked in the company office, I got to go on R & R twice during my stay in South Vietnam. The first time, in the fall of 1965, I returned to Okinawa. In the spring of the next year I went to, of all places, Saigon. I didn't consider it a safe haven, but at least it didn't require me to work during the day or stand guard duty at night.

For my first R & R, I managed to catch a jeep ride to the Da Nang airport, and once there I boarded a C-130 for the day's flight to Okinawa. No stranger to Okinawa, I had been stationed there twice, although the second time lasted only a few months before being transferred to South Vietnam. While stationed on Okinawa, I had been a typical, *Ugly American*, making my rabbit paths from base to bar. I failed to visit historical sights, learned very little about Okinawan culture, and did not make any effort to establish friendships with the island's inhabitants. I may not have been the first ugly American, but I fit the category, another one of my many regrets.

Such boorish behavior on my part bothers me to this day. Of course, I did come to know some of the Okinawan females who worked in bars and nightclubs. I tried to establish friendly relationships with them, and they taught me what little I knew of Okinawan culture. While on R & R, I re-visited my earlier haunts only to find that the girls I had known, without exception, had moved on to parts unknown. Prices had also changed, doubling for almost everything.

I had fond memories of Okinawa, going back to my first tour of duty there in 1963-64. Coming from a strict upbringing, I enjoyed the more relaxed and open environment found on the island. After WWII, many of the island's inhabitants were impoverished due to devastation caused by the war. An enterprising people, they learned that money could be made by providing entertainment and other services to American troops. Soon, bars and nightclubs sprang up all over the island, most near bases.

On the small island, prostitution and streetwalkers were not hard to find and were not illegal. In Kin Village, a small town outside Camp Hansen, where I spent my second tour of duty on the island, a local hotel provided the service—or so rumors had it. Entertainment in bars and nightclubs included no cover charge and hostesses were available who would sit and dance with you as long as you purchased drinks. Sometimes, bar girls and servicemen became romantically involved and would spend the night together after closing time. Thanks to over-night liberty, available to servicemen with good conduct, some Marines slept off base every night, an arrangement called "ranching." Of course, the bar girl would expect the Marine to pay the rent. In the early 1960s, a small apartment would run about sixty dollars a month. Again, that's what I've been told by other Marines.

During my three days in Okinawa, besides nightly visits to bars and nightclubs and sleeping late the following mornings, I spent daylight hours, getting pampered. For a few bucks, you could get a haircut, massage, and facial mudpack. Most of the barbers on Okinawa, all that

I can remember were female. I liked their gentle touch. The message, shoulders and back, came with the haircut at no extra charge.

In addition, steam baths were popular and inexpensive. The attendants at the steam bath were also female and, due to the nature of their work, wore only panties and bra. After one spent time in a steam-box, the attendant bathed *all* parts of one's body in a nonchalant manner. You were seated naked on a stool next to the bath tub. Only after you had been properly bathed and rinsed were you allowed to enter and soak in the tub. After soaking for a few minutes, you were dried off and given an all-over body massage. The massage included the ancient art of *ashiatsu*, massage by walking on the back.

For substance, I ate hamburgers and drank milkshakes at American-styled restaurants. The burgers and shakes were unheard of in war-torn South Vietnam. I avoided Asian food out of fear of the unfamiliar and my basic, teenage stupidity. While in Okinawa, I did eat fried rice, my only venture with Asian food. It could be ordered by phone and would be delivered to the barracks, like pizza delivery back in the states. The rice came in a thin, bamboo box with its top covered with a paper wrapper. I liked shrimp-fried rice, and I've never had better than what came in those bamboo boxes.

For lodging while on R&R, I stayed at a small, inexpensive hotel with few amenities. Despite the hotel's austerity, I appreciated the relaxed atmosphere and its worry-free environment. I could sleep without concern for in-coming rounds. The owner of the hotel, an elderly Okinawan lady, liked to be called, "mama-san." Besides being quite courteous, she expressed concern for my well-being in South Vietnam.

For older Okinawans, memories lingered of the horrors and harsh aftermath of WWII. Now, they were aware that most American troops fighting in South Vietnam were dispatched from Okinawa. Also, many bases on the island had stockpiles of supplies and munitions feeding the war effort. These activities caused many Okinawans to feel a sense of complicity in the deaths of other southeast Asians.

Nevertheless, because of relationships formed, most of the island's people still liked American GIs and expressed concern for our safety. At the same time, they wished that our bases on the island were located somewhere else.

My first night back in Okinawa, I re-visited a small bar located on coastal "Highway 1." Within walking distance of Camp Sukiran, the small bar remained in business and still looked the same. I had frequented the bar because of its close proximity. Some service men preferred to travel to entertainment strips were there were larger nightclubs. An abundance of small taxi cabs, which GIs called *s'koshi* cabs, were a cheap means of transportation. To the best of my memory, the small cabs charged a nickel for the first mile and fifteen cents for each mile after that. I'm told that Okinawans consider the cabs to be of normal size and resented them being called *s'koshi* by U.S. Military personnel.

I preferred to walk to the nearby bar and save cab fare for something else. I met a bar hostess who worked there and enjoyed her company, so I returned often. She looked nice and could dance very well. Plus, she did not try to hustle me to buy drinks in a hurry. I thought it would be fun to see her again, a nice surprise for both of us. It had been about two years since I saw her last. When I inquired about her, I was told that she had moved to Japan. I don't know if that was true or not. Okinawans were often leery about giving out personal information, due to the high GI crime rate on the island, including spats between GIs and their girlfriends. Many military personnel who lived with bar girls promised marriage but often left without even saying goodbye, hence the term "disposable girlfriends."

Bottom-line, the hostess I had known wasn't there, and I didn't recognize anyone else. That proved to be the case at all of the bars and nightclubs that I re-visited, and I returned to several. No one could, or would, tell me where the girls had moved on to. The girls I knew were gone, and prices were higher. It seemed that nothing remained the same, accept the appearance of the bars. Perhaps Thomas Wolfe had been correct, "You can't go home again."

Later, in the spring of '66, I had mixed emotions about the offer of R & R in Saigon. While I had never been to Saigon, I doubted that it would provide a relaxing environment. A fellow Marine told me that he had been there and had a good time. However, his steamy account of his experience didn't appeal to me. He told about visiting a bar and meeting an attractive hostess. He said she produced photos from her pocketbook, one at a time. The first photo showed her in a skimpy bikini. The second photo revealed her without a bra. In the third photo she appeared in the nude. Pleased with what he saw, he asked her how much a night with her would cost. After she told him, he asked to be excused, so he could go to the men's room.

Truth be told, he didn't need to relieve himself. He wanted to count his money in private and make sure he had enough. When he returned, he offered the money to the hostess. She said he had to pay the money to the club owners. After paying the owners, he followed behind her when the bar closed. She lived in a hotel on the outskirts of town. They got there by riding in separate pedicabs. He said he felt uneasy about the location. His concern proved to be justified. In the early morning hours, he said they were awakened by nearby machine-gun fire. He said he sat up in bed wondering what should they do? She spoke broken-English, but sitting up beside him, she placed her arm around his neck and reassured him.

"What's the matter? If we die, we die together."

"Well, that's mighty nice of you," he replied.

It seemed obvious that she had learned the phrase from another serviceman. Now, in perfect English, she used it on my friend. He said he had not been amused and wanted to tell her that she was crazy. My friend's tale did not appeal to me, so I decided to stick to the inner-city and stay by myself. I might not have had much fun, but I welcomed the break in action and change of activity.

During the day, giving in to my curiosity and mustering my courage, I shopped in the city's open markets. I spent more time looking than buying. I did purchase a pair of onyx cuff links with an inset of two Asian letters made of mother-of-pearl. I have no idea what the lettering meant. For all I know they may have spelled out, "Ugly American." I also bought a marble carving of a panther about eight or nine inches in length. I must have had good taste, or at least someone thought so. When I returned to the states, both items were stolen.

Truth be told, I don't remember much about my Saigon excursion. I didn't do anything out of the ordinary. I did try some Vietnamese noodles. I had heard stories about VC lobbing grenades into restaurants, so I made sure to sit far to the back. With so many people milling about, you never knew if the enemy might be nearby or even standing next to you. Besides being crowded, the city had a nighttime curfew. During the night shooting and shelling could be heard in the distance.

Years later, while a graduate student at The University of Georgia, and with the war still in progress, other students and I attended a meeting with a respected U.S. Senator. Having just returned from a fact-finding mission to South Vietnam, the senator assured students that the news media's reports of the war not going well were not true. I couldn't believe my ears, with the war now in its second decade, how could that not be bad? Did the senator dispute all the negative news reports I had seen on television? Could they all be wrong?

He stated, "I've just been on the streets of Saigon, and the people there were going about their business without any concern."

Well, whoop-teed-do, I thought.

I had been on the streets of Saigon and had a different opinion. I knew the streets weren't safe. In the past, in broad daylight, VC riding by on motorbikes had thrown grenades into restaurants frequented by Americans. At nighttime, gunfire could be heard in different parts of the city. Either the senator had a political bias or he had had been duped by his handlers. With my limited experience, I knew that in daytime, people went about their business in their usual manner because they had no choice. Even during time of war, people's livelihood depended on earning money or food items, etc. It's what the common working people do to survive.

Also, VC were not known to attack Vietnamese at random. Rather, they targeted Americans, political opponents, and ARVN soldiers. As for the safety of the streets, you were required by law to be off them at night, so the ARVN could detect any movement by the Viet Cong. The VC, outfitted in civilian clothes, blended unnoticed into Saigon's daytime activity on its *safe* streets. Also, I doubt the senator ventured outside the inner-city of Saigon were safety could not be guaranteed.

While I knew the senator's remarks weren't accurate, I didn't argue his point. Being a grad student, my word against that of a U.S. Senator wouldn't carry much weight. After all, the senator served on the U.S. Senate Committee on Armed Services. He had respected political credentials and had been to South Vietnam on a fact-finding mission. That made him a foreign affairs expert. I had only 10 months of experience in South Vietnam. My credentials didn't measure up. Still, the passing of time proved me right. I take no satisfaction in that. Well, I'm human, so I do.

Chapter 10

Mortar/Infantry Attack

August 9, 1965 is a date I'll always remember. We had been in South Vietnam for a month or so. On that date, I had been assigned to guard duty. That evening I reported to the Corporal of the Guard for my assignment. I learned that I had been assigned to the bunker designated as the "right 50." I told the corporal that I had been assigned to that bunker four times in a row. I argued that we were supposed to rotate from one bunker to another in order to become familiar with each.

It wasn't much of an argument. We had been on Hill 34 long enough that I had been assigned to all of our bunkers and knew their layouts quite well. Further more, I had helped construct them. Still, I had a personal reason for wanting my assignment changed to another bunker, and I insisted on fair treatment. I knew the Marine who had been assigned Corporal of the Guard duty that night. He and I were not the best of friends. I doubted he would change my assignment, but to my surprise he did.

Two Marines were assigned to each bunker, so that by rotating sack time, the two of them would both be able to get some sleep during the night. When arriving at their assigned bunker, neither Marine would be sleepy. At some point during late evening hours, one of the two would decide to get some shut-eye on the cot placed to the rear of the bunker. Thus, a two-hour shift of on-and-off guard duty would commence. The awake Marine would remain on guard behind the machine-gun and keep watch for enemy movement through the bunker's aperture.

After two hours, the Marine on watch would wake the other Marine. He would then take his two-hour turn on the cot. And, so it went, two hours on and two hours off throughout the night until 0600 hours the next morning. Of course, having your sleep interrupted every two hours made you feel like you'd had no sleep at all. When you reported to work, after a night of interrupted sleep, you felt felt haggard for the remainder of the day. Somehow we managed to labor through the day, and later that night we didn't go to sleep. We collapsed into oblivion.

More than sleep deprivation impacted my dislike for the "right 50" bunker. Each morning when leaving that bunker for work, one of the two Marines would have to carry the .50 caliber machine-gun to the armory tent and clean and oil it. After cleaning, the gun would then be returned and wrapped in a poncho. That ensured that when other Marines reported to the bunker later that day, they would have a clean weapon at their disposal. Also, the daily cleaning and oiling helped protect the gun from possible jams due to sand and from developing rust caused by the humid, semi-tropical weather.

The bunkers were usually manned by privates, privates first class, and lance/corporals. Once in a blue moon, a corporal might be needed to fill-in, but most of the time, a lance/corporal would be in charge. Being a lance/corporal, I had the privilege of assigning the cleaning of the bunker's machine gun to the other Marine of lesser rank. However, being a nice guy, I couldn't bring myself to dump the task off on someone else. We were both tired at the end of our duty. I didn't want to be resented by a fellow Marine, so I handled the unpleasant chore myself.

The cleaning of the .50-caliber did not bother me, but it's weight did. My dislike had to due with carrying the weapon cradled in my arms for a long distance. I estimate the trip from bunker to armory tent to have been in excess of 100 yards. Once the weapon had been cleaned, it had to be carried back and put in place in the bunker. That's a rather unpleasant task when you're tired and feeling haggard.

The automatic weapons in the other bunkers were much lighter. Having lugged the .50-caliber several times, I did not relish doing it again. Therefore, I complained to the Corporal of the Guard about my assignment. Of course, I didn't bother to mention that I only objected due to the weight of the weapon. The corporal bought my lame excuse about familiarization and reassigned me to another bunker, the "left 60." A lance/corporal in the "left 60" got transferred to my previous assignment in the "right 50." I felt relieved. My relief would be short-lived and turn into remorse.

Sometime after 2300 hours, I found it difficult to keep my eyes open. The problem with that had to do with the fact that my fellow Marine lie asleep on the cot, and he had another hour or so before relieving me. I needed some caffeine, to help keep me awake. Lucky for me, coffee could be had at the "CP bunker" about 20 or 30 yards away. If I hurried it would not take long for me to get some and return..

Each night one of the Marines on guard-duty stopped by the mess tent to pick up a cooler full of coffee. The well-insulated cooler, provided by food services, kept things hot as well as cool. We did not have thermoses, but the cooler served just as well and held enough coffee for everyone on guard duty. Before leaving the bunker to obtain coffee, I should have awakened the Marine asleep on the cot. Not wanting to interrupt his sleep, I decided not to do that. I didn't intend to be gone but just long enough to dip my canteen cup into the cooler and then return. It would be a quick trip, Besides, what could go wrong in just a minute or two? I'd soon find out.

The "CP bunker" set atop the hill, offering a sweeping view of the expanse of rice paddies and bamboo thickets below and for miles out in front. To provide a modicum of protection, a waste-high wall of sandbags had been positioned directly in front of the bunker, which had an open doorway facing its southern view of the area. The cooler of coffee had been set off to one side of the bunker.

In haste, I made my way to the "CP bunker," and opened the lid to the cooler. After filling my canteen cup, I stopped to speak to the staff-sergeant on duty. He stood in front of the bunker, behind the sandbagged wall. Like me, he came from the South and had a relaxed manner. Standing next to him, we spoke to each other in hushed voices. Just when I started to leave, out in front of us, across the rice paddies along the edge of the bamboo thicket, were several bright flashes. I counted 10 or 12, about 20 to 30 feet apart. I wondered if I had just witnessed "short rounds," but then I heard a warble sound in the air. The sound kept getting louder instead of softer.

The easy going sergeant, a Korean War veteran, said, in an excited voice, **"It's in-coming**!" Out of reaction to his words, I turned to him but found myself all alone. The sergeant had disappeared. After giving his urgent warning, in a millisecond he had dashed inside the "CP bunker," leaving me standing flat-footed and dumbfounded. With the warbling sound getting louder, I realized I needed to get back to my assigned post. I turned and made a hasty retreat in direction of the "left 60." Before I could make it back to the bunker, I could hear mortar rounds hitting behind me. I feared I might not be able to out run them. I shifted into my highest gear. I've never run faster.

Upon reaching the trench close to the bunker's entrance, I dove down into it. I grabbed my fellow Marine's helmet in passing. He had left it sitting just outside the bunker on the trench's top edge. When I entered the bunker, my partner, awakened by the noise of the mortars, set upright on the cot. He gave me a quizzical look that implied, *What's going on?* Without saying a word, I tossed him his helmet and jumped behind our M60 machine-gun.

The enemy's mortars first hit the right corner, facing south, of our hill. Then the mortar fire walked across the front of the hill, before spreading back throughout the camp's tent area. We had been warned that Viet Cong would often charge behind their mortar barrage. Sometimes, they would even invade a position with the mortars, taking the risk of being hit by their own fire, in order to catch servicemen with their heads pinned down.

I loaded the M60 with belt-ammo and slammed a round into the gun's chamber. My right index finger rested against the trigger ready to squeeze and fire a hail of bullets into the enemy. I disliked fighting, but I disliked the thought of dying even more. I watched and waited for VC to charge up the hill, ready to kill all that I could. Instead a bright yellow flash filled my view. Sand and small rocks rained into the bunker through it's aperture.

The concussion of the mortar made a *woo-sh* sound, which remains imprinted in my memory. A mortar had struck in front of our bunker. I guess the embedded granite rock and the incline of the hill caused the mortar's shrapnel to spread horizontally and fly into the base of our sand-bagged bunker. That's a guess. I'm not sure what saved us from the deadly shrapnel. Instead of razor-sharp metal, a pebble struck my forehead causing a small bump. I did not bleed, the skin had not been broken. There would be no purple heart awarded, and for that I am thankful. If it had been shrapnel instead of a pebble, it would have sliced through my brain, and you wouldn't be reading this memoir.

Concerned that standing behind the machine gun, centered in the bunker's aperture, might not be the safest thing to do, I ordered my fellow Marine to stand to one side of the opening and look out in front to the left. On the other side of the machine-gun, I would stand and look out in front to the right. That way we both could see the entire area in front and have some protection from rifle fire or mortar shrapnel. Of course, if VC stormed the hill, I would need to jump back behind the M60 and open fire. Otherwise, we would hold our positions and remain to some extent protected from frontal hits. That may not sound brave, but, again, you can't kill the enemy if you're dead.

When the mortar barrage ended, I heard nothing but silence. Soon a wave of moaning swept the hill, followed by desperate cries for "corpsmen." That's when I realized that fellow Marines had been wounded. For some fatalistic reason, I felt if we were ever attacked, I would be a casualty. I don't know why I felt that way, but I did. It amazed me to still be alive, when others had suffered serious injury and some where now dead. I learned the next day that we had four Marines killed and 24 wounded. The lance/corporal who had been transferred to my "right 50" assignment took a direct hit. He didn't survive. Had I not complained to the Corporal of the Guard, he would have lived instead of me. I had no way of knowing what would happen that night. I have nothing else to say about that, except I knew him. I liked him, and his death saddens me still.

The next day, we went back to our job assignments like nothing had happened. Within two days, I would be back on guard duty. In an ironic twist, I got transferred from my job in Shop Stores to that of fiscal clerk, processing copies of requisitions, invoices, and receipts. I replaced the Marine who had taken my place in the "right 50." Life can be a cruel mistress.

Following the mortar attack, I wondered why our tanks had not entered the fray. I learned, to my dismay, our tank crews had to get permission from division headquarters before firing in the direction of the hamlet in front of us. The communication system required the tankers to go through different relays in order to reach 9th Marines HQ. By the time tankers got through to division headquarters, the mortar barrage had ended. The next day, the commander of The Third Marine Division, a three-star general, visited our camp. He surveyed the situation and talked with the tankers. He told them the next time we came under attack they would not need permission to return fire. I welcomed the general's decision, but I regretted that it had not come sooner, and I hoped there would be no next time.

A week or two later, while off-duty in my sleeping quarters, all hell broke lose. Gun fire erupted from the front and both sides of our camp. I rolled off my cot onto the tent's floor. I had been listening to my portable radio. Still dressed in my work utilities, I struggled to put on my boots, cartridge belt, and flak jacket. I grabbed my rifle and put on my helmet. Peering outside, I could see tracer rounds crisscrossing through the air.

In military-issued ammo, every fourth round is coated in phosphorus. When fired, those rounds glow yellow and can be seen in the dark. It helps the shooter determine where his rounds are hitting. On the down side, it gives away the shooter's position. A rapid rate of fire of makes the phosphorus rounds look like a steady stream. The crisscrossing gun fire reminded me of movie films I had seen of the "London Blitzkrieg." When the firing stopped, someone beat on the artillery shell hanging by chain outside the CO's tent. That was the signal for all troops not on guard duty to go to their assigned trench area on the camp's perimeter.

The Marines manning the bunkers, our three tanks and the Ontos unit, held back the attackers, and now the rest of us would go up and fill-in the trenches in case the VC regrouped and mounted a second attack. I raced toward the front of the hill, ahead of all others. Hidden behind clouds, the moon provided no illumination. I made my way forward in the dark. At least, the moonless night helped to conceal me from enemy eyes. I kept running forward, and someone in a tent challenged me.

"Halt, who goes there?"

The voice came from a tent smaller than a GP tent. Its occupant had to be an officer, or a senior NCO, a Marine superior in rank to me. I wondered, had he not heard the alarm, or does he think that I might be a VC? Either way, I didn't have time or inclination to discuss the matter.

I yelled out, "Headed to the front. You need to get your ass in gear."

I didn't wait for a reply. Whatever rank he held, I thought him to be dim-witted and continued running, appreciative that my identity had been masked by the absent moon. Nearing the crest of the hill, I had a decision to make. Should I just run over the hilltop, making myself into a silhouetted target, or get down and crawl over terrain littered with bits of rock? I didn't like either choices, and I had to do one or the other in order to reach the trench on the down-hill side. Then I heard the footsteps of another Marine closing behind me. I slowed so that he could catch up.

"Are you okay?" he asked when beside me.

"I'm fine, just needed to catch my breath," I replied, motioning for him to go on. After he passed me, I ran even slower and listened. Soon, he disappeared over the crest, and I heard no shooting. With the absence of gunfire, I decided to take the chance and run over instead of crawling. Still somewhat of a risk, but I believed my odds had now improved. I admit having some guilt for using the other Marine as bait. However, I felt certain that he would run not crawl, so it made sense to me to wait and learn his fate before tempting mine. You may think less of me for it, but I'm reminded of the saying, *All's Fair in Love and War*. Besides, it seemed the smart thing to do.

Once in the trench, I fixed my bayonet to my rifle. I hoped that my ammo wouldn't give out, but I needed to be ready if it did. Next to shooting someone, using my bayonet and hand-to-hand combat were actions I dreaded the most. I wish I had been without fear, but I admit to being scared. I wanted other Marines in the trench to move closer, closing the interval between us. Truth be told, I doubt we were more than five or six feet apart, but at that moment it seemed that we were much more distant. Fear can cloud your judgment of such matters. Waiting for the enemy to charge, bitter reflux came up in throat, no doubt caused by anxiety or fear or both.

The shooting did not resume. In a desperate attempt to draw enemy fire, our company gunnery sergeant, not the sharpest stick in the pile, ran back and forth just below the crest of the hill. He waved the small flame from his Zippo lighter, trying to attract the enemy's attention. In my opinion, if he had been shot he would have deserved it. I think some career military welcome a fight. While the overzealous sergeant tried to draw enemy fire, I had a different desire. I wanted to be left alone.

After the mortar and infantry attacks, we expected more to follow. However, we would lose no more men or experience any more assaults during the remainder of my stay on Hill 34. We were out of danger, except for periodic sniper fire. Of course, we had no way of knowing that. Off in the distance, gunfire could still be heard most days and nights. It served to remind us of imminent danger, so stress remained a daily companion. And, God forbid, with his repeated attempts, the sniper's aim might improve.

Chapter 11

Counting Down

In my final month, I drew up a short-timer's calendar. To keep it simple, I sketched a combat boot and divided it into 31 sections. I posted the calendar at my work station. Each day I filled-in a section, starting with the highest number. Soon, my departure date would arrive. I had mixed feelings due to leaving friends behind. Marines report to new duty stations on an individual basis, at different dates. A Marine buddy may have joined your outfit four months after your arrival. Thus, when rotating out after your 13th month, you would be leaving your friend behind. Other friends who arrived before you also left before you, leaving you behind. Adding more complexity to the mix, even if you served a twenty-year career in the Marine Corps, since you and your friends received orders at different times and often to different bases, you might never see each other again. In the military, you lived in the moment because friendships tended to drift apart.

Still, I looked forward to leaving and, at the same time, became anxious about it. I heard of other Marines being killed just days before or even on their departure date. One evening I left my GP tent, needing to fill my canteen from the water-buffalo parked nearby. At some point, I realized I had ventured off in the wrong direction. I felt a disoriented but somehow managed to re-direct myself back to my tent. I tried to relax on my cot, hoping to calm my nerves, but I felt no better. After awhile and still feeling uneasy, I told a fellow Marine that I needed to go to the medical tent. I asked him, in the event I didn't return by the next morning, to let my superiors at work know where I had gone. Now dark, I soon found myself using a flashlight to find my way. I walked quite a ways shining the light in the darkness before I came to my senses.

It dawned on me, *What am I doing using a flashlight? I could get shot.*

I knew that my actions were strange but did not understand the origins of my difficulty. At last, I made it to the medical tent where a corpsman remained on duty. I don't remember if he offered me any medicine, but he did have me spend the night on an available cot. Somehow I managed to go to sleep.

The next morning, the camp's doctor, a naval captain, examined me. He determined that I had experienced an acute anxiety reaction made worse by dehydration. Again, I don't remember if I had been given medicine, but I do remember the doctor telling me to drink water often and take salt tablets.

I remember thinking, how's that going to help my nerves?

I returned to work that same morning and don't recall having anymore problems. Since I didn't take the salt tablets, it seemed that increasing my water intake made all the difference. Who knew water would cure anxiety? Then, some people think a few drops on the head during baptism makes you right with God. In my opinion, water does not have magical powers. It's only good for drinking, bathing, washing, and watering grass and plants. Oh yeah, and fish seem to like it. I prefer bourbon, straight up.

Chapter 12

Homecoming

On my departure date, sometime early May of 1966, I flew on a C-130 from South Vietnam's Da Nang Air Base to the Kadena Air Force Base in Okinawa. The C-130, a lumbering cargo/troop carrier, had fold-down seats mounted on its sides. The seats were not comfortable and could not be adjusted. You set facing the persons on the other side of the aircraft, not a scenic view. Also, condensation would form on the plane's ceiling and, from time to time, drip onto passengers below.

Nevertheless, I much preferred flying by C-130 to sailing by slow ship. After a few hours flight, we landed at Kadena. I would spend four days on Okinawa before departing. By a change of luck, I got switched to a modern Boeing 747. Seated on the sleek, four-engine jet plane, I felt like a first-class passenger on holiday rather than a low-ranked Marine in transit. We would fly non-stop to the Naval Air Base at Barber's Point, Hawaii. From there we would fly on to San Diego. Alas, I had returned intact to the United States of America. I had survived the war, and, unlike many others, I knew I would not have to return.

I suppose college students were the first to protest against the Vietnam War. However, upon my arrival, there were no protesters to jeer me. Being the early part of the war, they had not yet organized. In fact, I had no welcoming party of any kind. I had orders to report to Camp Pendleton, a Marine Corps infantry training base, now also a staging and receiving station. Pendleton processed Marines headed to war and those returning from it. With no transportation provided, I had to catch a cab to get there. I would remain at Camp Pendleton for a few days before before receiving my assignment to my next duty station.

Having been overseas for over a year, I qualified for a 30-day leave, but I declined it in order to complete active-duty as soon as possible. In fact, I should have been able to take the leave and be discharged from the Marine Corps while at Camp Pendleton. My four-year enlistment ended on 30 June, but my discharge date had changed. Due to difficulty recruiting personnel for the Marine Corps, President Lyndon Johnson extended all Navy and Marine Corps enlistments for six months. Thus, I had to report to a new duty station in order to complete the extension.

Since I worked in supply, it did not surprise me to receive orders to report to the Marine Corps Supply Center located in Albany, Georgia. I had been stationed there prior to heading back to Okinawa for my second tour on the island, cut short by a division transfer to South Vietnam. While stationed in Albany, I had been nominated for "Marine of the Month," and promoted to lance/corporal. Also, that year I won a new 1964 Volkswagen in a raffle.

In order to raise money for needy service families, the Marine Corps and the Navy, once a year sold tickets and raffled off prizes. The top prize being a new car. At larger facilities, like Camp Lejeune located in North Carolina, the new car would be a Cadillac. I had no complaints about winning the much cheaper Volkswagen. Due to its better gas mileage, it would be a more appropriate fit for my salary range.

I would not have won the Volkswagen without the help of a kind sergeant. The sergeant like other senior NCOs sold the raffle tickets on base to other Marines. I had no intention of buying any of the tickets because I didn't have good luck at gambling. There had been an insufficient sale of the tickets, so the sale had been extended for three months. On the final day of the extension, the sergeant approached me and asked if I would purchase the last two books of tickets that he had remaining. The books of tickets sold for $1.50 each. I don't remember how many tickets were in a book. I suppose not many. At any rate, being that I had just been paid, I took pity on the sergeant and purchased the two books. After I paid, the sergeant tried to hand me the tickets, I refused to accept them.

"Sarge, I don't have any luck at gambling. Why don't you just add my money to what you've made so far, and see if you can sell the tickets to some other Marine," I suggested.

The sergeant went back to his desk, and, without telling me, he filled out my name and rank on the ticket stubs. He then left the warehouse where we worked and deposited the ticket stubs into the barrel located by the entrance door to the base's administration building. A few days later our Commanding General drew out the winning ticket stub. That's how I acquired a new, 1964 red Volkswagen sedan, my very first car!

Upon my return to Albany from South Vietnam, once again, I met with good fortune. After a month, I received recommendation for "Marine of the Quarter." Along with three other recommended Marines, I interviewed before a panel of officers and senior-ranked sergeants. One question I remember being asked had to do with me being in a transport truck leading a convoy, and if we came under fire what would I tell the driver?

I replied that I hoped I wouldn't have to tell him anything. If I did, it would be to speed up. I think they thought that I might order the driver to stop, get out of the truck and set up a hasty defense. I explained that the enemy would already have the area zeroed-in, and the ditches would most likely be full of punji stakes. If we stopped we would be sitting ducks. I preferred to keep going and live to fight another day, under more favorable circumstances. I reasoned that if we drove on and hit a mine in the road, at least we would have cleared the way for the remainder of the convoy. There were other similar questions. Another that I recall, they asked if I went out on a night ambush what kind of defense would I set up. They seemed obsessed with kinds of defenses.

I gave a short reply, "If I were back in Vietnam, a 360 degree one."

My answer may not have reflected types of defenses found in the Marine Corps Guidebook, but I spoke from experience. The panel of career Marines must have liked my answers. They selected me above the others to be "Marine of the Quarter." Again, I didn't seek recognition. I only stayed "squared away" in order to keep senior staff off my back. I repeat, I just wanted to be left alone. Somehow, the Marine Corps never got the message.

Our base commander, a brigadier general, awarded me a meritorious promotion to sergeant E-5. A little more than a year earlier, the same general pulled my ticket from a barrel of raffle tickets. That's when I won the new, 1964 red Volkswagen sedan. In another twist of fate, several years later after I had reentered civilian life, the general's son would become my children's pediatrician. A good doctor and a nice guy, I couldn't help but tease him a little.

I told the doctor, "I don't know how your dad treated you, but he gave me a new car and extra spending money."

To be honest, I had some good times in the Marine Corps, made a few friends and traveled overseas. Overall though, military life didn't appeal to me, especially the combat part. When I returned to the states from the stressful conditions of South Vietnam, there had been no psychological evaluation, no consideration of emotional stress, and no counseling.

My superiors seemed to expect me to just flip a switch, turning the war off and turning normal life back on. Without any delay, they required me to report to work, business as usual. I don't believe the insensitive treatment to have been intentional. At that time, I doubt there had been any thought given to what support might be needed for returning veterans. I hope the homecoming reception improved for others who returned later. A survey conducted by the Veterans Administration concluded, 500,000 of the 3 million troops who fought in South Vietnam suffered from post-traumatic stress disorder.

Following my discharge from active duty, I had a few nightmares of being attacked by VC. I also dreamed of being stuck in the Marine Corps, frozen in rank and unable to get out. In reality, the president canceled the six-month extension after three months and a few days. He did so after a sufficient increase in troop levels. Once an all-volunteer branch of military service, the Marine Corps started drafting troops and soon met its quota. Thus, with the extension canceled in October of 1966, I returned to civilian life. I had completed four years, three months, 6 days, 14 hours, and 47 seconds in the Marine Corps. My obligated time had been served. After a few months of waiting for the start of a new semester, I enrolled in college. My path had come full-circle, and I had answered the question, posed by American poet, Langston Hughes: "What happens to a dream deferred."

Chapter 13

Opposition

I trust I've made my disdain for war clear. Be not misled, many others besides myself opposed our involvement in South Vietnam. I wish to address that opposition because I don't want readers, too young to remember the Vietnam era, to think the war went unopposed or to not know how much it divided our nation, lest it happen again.

Also, I think it's fitting to include this chapter in my memoir because, while enrolled in college, yours truly led a one-man, heated demonstration opposing U.S. Military involvement in South Vietnam.

In 1968, I attended a senior college in conservative, south Georgia. All the heat, including threats of injury, came from students, among hundreds of them, who did not agree with my point of view. I had survived the horrors of Vietnam only to be threatened with harm by fellow college students.

Truth be told, many of those students were draft dodgers, utilizing college deferment to avoid the war. I found it strange that they voiced support for U.S. Military involvement in South Vietnam but did not choose to participate in the fighting. The students voicing support of the war effort at this Deep South college were atypical of college students in other regions throughout America. At most American colleges and universities, students—in overwhelming numbers—opposed U.S. Military involvement in South Vietnam.

There's no logical rationale to be had with some people. On that day, I faced students whose reasoning seemed to me to be convoluted and flawed. Not one to seek limelight, I had let my emotions get the better of me. In so doing, I had placed myself at the forefront of confrontation. I will address that further, but first I think it's important to begin with why America came to commit U.S. Armed Forces to South Vietnam.

Quite often in our nation's history, persons or groups, with special interests or hidden agendas, have orchestrated our involvement in war. Older men in power seem hell bent on sending younger men into harm's way. It's a trend repeated too often to ignore. Sometimes their actions might be legitimate but often times not. An argument can be made that our involvement in South Vietnam began due to legitimate concerns about the spread of communism in Southeast Asia.

Others argued that South Vietnam's civil unrest did not any way endanger the United States. They claimed that our involvement amounted to no more than a Neo-nationalistic effort to spread American influence and dominate other nations, while favoring America's Capitalist corporations.

During election years, corporations contribute millions of dollars to presidential and congressional campaigns in order to curry favor. Alas, the truth behind U.S. Military intervention in Vietnam may allude us, but what follows is a brief history of it.

In May 1954, French troops were defeated in the Battle of Dien Bien Phu by the Viet Minh, Ho Chi Minh's Communist inspired army. The French then withdrew all of their military forces out of Indochina. Later that year, at the Geneva Convention, the regions of Indochina were divided into four countries: North Vietnam, South Vietnam, Cambodia, and Laos.

Fearing the spread of communism, in 1955 U.S. President Dwight D. Eisenhower pledged firm support to South Vietnam. Eisenhower, a former five-star Army general, popularized *The Domino Theory*. The theory predicted that if one country fell to communism other neighboring countries would then fall in succession. In his farewell address of January 1961, Eisenhower warned of the detrimental effects of the *Military-*

Industrial Complex, the close relationship between government and defense contractors which influences public policy. Eisenhower had begun to resent pressure from defense contractors to increase our involvement in the South Vietnam war effort. During Ike's time in office, about 900 American troops were assigned to South Vietnam.

In the early 1960s Eisenhower's successor, John F. Kennedy, likewise intervened in South Vietnam to ensure the South Vietnamese domino didn't fall. Further, Kennedy believed that the communist-led Pathet Lao in Laos would be able, with assistance from the Viet Cong, to take over Laos. Later, President Kennedy had a change in his thinking, due to the ineptitude and corruption of the Saigon government and its refusal to make reforms. Before his assassination in November of 1963, he had begun a limited recall of U.S. Military forces. During JFK's administration, American troop strength in South Vietnam increased to 16,000.

On the other hand, Kennedy's successor, Lyndon B. Johnson, supported escalation of U.S. Military involvement in South Vietnam to thwart what he perceived to be the Soviet Union's expansionist policies. A provocation by three North Vietnamese Navy torpedo boats aided Johnson's desire to escalate. In August 2nd of 1964, three enemy torpedo boats engaged the U.S. Destroyer USS Maddox with torpedo and machine-gun fire. The Maddox had been performing a signals intelligence patrol off the coast of North Vietnam. Again, on August 4th USS Maddox reported a second sea battle.

Both of the reported attacks occurred in the Gulf of Tonkin, hence the name, *Gulf of Tonkin Incident*. There is no evidence that a second attack occurred, only recorded images of "Tonkin Ghosts," false radar signals. It should also be noted that there were no casualties in either of the two reported attacks. Still, based on the claim of the two attacks, Congress granted President Johnson legal authority to deploy U.S. Military forces in open warfare against North Vietnam. Given the lack of fatalities in the Gulf of Tonkin Incident, one can't help but wonder if members of Congress had been influenced by defense contractors. Later Johnson, in a joking manner, admitted that during the second attack the Navy might have been shooting at whales. During LBJ's time in office, U.S. troop strength in South Vietnam increased to 536,100.

A recap of the increase in America's troop strength in South Vietnam, registers the following numbers: 900 during the Eisenhower administration, 16,000 during the Kennedy administration, and 536,100 during the Johnson administration. In the early years of the intervention, most Americans supported to war effort. Those in support came to be called, "Hawks," and those opposed were called, "Doves." Much resentment and animosity existed between the two groups.

The draft, a system of conscription used for recruitment for the South Vietnam war effort, had its beginning in May of 1965. With the privileged class being given college deferments, the draft drew most of its young men from minorities and lower and middle class whites. Records show that 80 percent of troops that served in South Vietnam came from the lower classes. College enrollments swelled to a record number of 9 million by the end of the 1960s. Even privileged, male students needed to remain in college beyond their 26th birthday in order to avoid being drafted. In a show of defiance, some of the college students burned their draft cards. Issues with the draft drove much of the protests after 1965.

When the number of injuries and deaths of U.S. Military personnel mounted, support for the war effort dwindled. For the first time in history, battlefield action—injuries and fatalities—were recorded by war correspondents embedded with the U.S. Military. Their films and photographs were shown each night on TV's evening news. Those telecasts brought the horror of war home to American's viewing audience. The numbers reported were no longer static figures. They took on a life of their own, both shocking and sad. By 1967, U.S. casualties reached 15,058 killed and 109,527 wounded.

In July of 1967, President Johnson doubled the number of men drafted per month from 17,000 to 35,000. Soon after, he signed a bill making it illegal to burn a draft card. To avoid conscription, 30,000 young Americans left the country, moving to Canada, Sweden, Japan, and Mexico. Others joined the National Guard or the Peace Corps in order to escape the draft. In October of 1967, 35,000 demonstrators protested against the Vietnam War outside the Pentagon.

Perhaps no other incident turned Americans against the Vietnam war effort than the one that occurred in March of 1968. That incident is so repulsive that I don't care to go into detail about it. What I will tell you is that some U.S Army soldiers, frustrated by casualties within their ranks, went on a rampage in the South Vietnamese village of My Lai. The village males, suspected of being Viet Cong sympathizers, were alerted to the Army's impending arrival, and were not present. Nevertheless, the American soldiers slaughtered about 500 unarmed women, children, babies, and older Vietnamese unable to flee or defend themselves. *The My Lai Incident* amounted to horrific acts of rape and murder committed by American servicemen on innocent civilians.

In the spring of 1968, following the massacre at My Lai, members of the organization, Students for a Democratic Society (SDS) called for colleges across American to stage "Ten Days of Resistance," consisting of rallies, marches, sit-ins—any form of protest against U.S. military involvement in South Vietnam. I did not hold membership in SDS or any other protest group. Nevertheless, I had feelings of guilt for not doing anything in a public way to denounce the war effort. I decided to demonstrate on my own. On poster board I wrote the phrase, "Immediate Withdrawal." Had I been more Hemingway-like, and relied on simple words, I might have coined the slogan that later became popular, "Out Now."

Early the next class day, armed with my poster, I ascended the steps to the platform of our college's student center. I paced from one side of the student center midway to its entrance. Not wanting to impede the coming or going of anyone, I turned at the doorway and walked back to the side from which I came. I held my poster in front of me for all to see. I continued my one-man protest for three or four hours, saying nothing while walking back and forth. By that time, a crowd of students, numbering in the hundreds, had gathered in front of the building. It became clear that those students did not share my anti-war view. Some knuckleheads in the crowd yelled at me with threats of injury. I ignored their threats and continued my protest demonstration, pacing back and forth.

I did have some support in the crowd. About 10 or 15 students, classmates from my speech and drama classes, in a show of solidarity, came up onto the student center platform and stood against the wall behind me. When I decided to end my demonstration, one of those students approached me and asked if I would assume the leadership of those students against the Vietnam War. I thanked the student for the offer, but I declined.

I told him, "I'm sorry, man. I'm not a leader or a follower. I just do my own thing."

In November of 1969, the largest anti-war demonstration in the history of the United States occurred in Washington, D.C. Frustrated by the lack of progress, mounting casualties, and high cost of the war effort, an estimated 250,000 Americans gathered together, calling for the withdrawal of all American troops from South Vietnam.

Early in 1970, the U.S. military and South Vietnamese forces conducted a joint invasion of Cambodia, followed by an invasion of Laos by South Vietnamese troops. The South Vietnamese were pushed back out of Laos by forces from North Vietnam. The expansion of the war effort beyond the boundaries of South Vietnam resulted in a new wave of protests on American college campuses.

One such protest occurred at Kent State University located at the town of Kent, about 40 miles south of Cleveland. Over the course of four days, unruly protests occurred in town and on the campus.

In town, storefront windows were broken and some people in the crowd started a small bonfire in the street. On campus, protesters set the ROTC building afire. The mayor of the town met with university officials. They made the decision to call the state's governor and request that National Guard troops be sent to assist in controlling the protesters.

Some of the National Guard troops that arrived on campus were the same age or not much older than the college students. The troops and the students represented a cultural divide. The troops may have resented the students and their privileged status. Not well-trained, the guardsmen were rattled by protesters throwing rocks and yelling insults. Without warning—29 of the 77 guard members—fired upon the students killing four and wounding nine others. Two of the students killed were three hundred yards away from the guardsmen, the total length of three football fields. They were not protesters, just by-standers, watching the demonstration from afar during a break in their classes.

In April of 1971, Vietnam veterans threw away 700 Vietnam service medals on the steps of the nation's Capitol building. The next day 500,000 Americans marched in protest. The tide of public opinion had changed. Americans by a large majority now opposed U.S. Military involvement in South Vietnam. Like never before, citizens began to pressure the President and Congress for the complete withdrawal of American troops from the Far East war.

In June of 1973, the U.S. and North Vietnam concluded a final peace agreement. During more than two decades of fighting, two million Vietnamese were killed, three million wounded, and 12 million became refugees. American troops suffered over 50,000 deaths. Soon after American troops withdrew, South and North Vietnam were united into one country under communist rule. Despite political differences, the United States and Vietnam now do business together, and American tourists visit Vietnam on a frequent basis.

Afterword

When I served in the U.S. Marine Corps, every Marine had volunteered. Later during the escalation of the Vietnam War, after I had returned to the states, the Marine Corps started accepting draftees. I can't speak to the fervor of the drafted Marines. I did not serve with them, but as far as I know, they preformed with honor.

While I made fun of Marines in this memoir, including officers, it was done in jest. The vast majority of the Marines I served with in Vietnam were noble and brave, their patriotism beyond reproach. Units of Third Tank Battalion were awarded the Navy Presidential Unit Citation. The award is given to units for extraordinary heroism in action against an armed enemy.

The collective degree of valor (combat heroism) against an armed enemy by the unit nominated for the Presidential Unit Citation is the same as that which would warrant award of the individual award of the Distinguished Service Cross, Air Force Cross or Navy Cross.

Despite the anti-war sentiment expressed in this memoir, which I embrace without apology, I do recognize that there are times when war is inevitable. Such drastic course of action should only be undertaken—as common sense dictates—when all other avenues of reason and diplomacy have failed.

Supporting countries and dictators to prevent the spread of communism when such heads of state are corrupt and violent towards their own people and their political opponents is quite often counterproductive. Likewise, sending American troops into harm's way in order to exploit another country's resources should never be permitted. And, invading other nations in order for American companies and corporations to expand their global outreach is repugnant and should not be allowed.

All of the aforementioned actions have been undertaken by our military in the past at the direction of congress and with approval of presidents. Such impropriety should be repudiated by the American public. My admonitions sound simple enough, but the most difficult part of world affairs is knowing the truth, and when learning the truth knowing how to act on it. It's not an easy proposition.

Let me leave you with this quote from *Rosencrantz and Guildenstern Are Dead*:

GUIL: We only know what we're told, and that's little enough.

And for all we know it isn't even true.

PLAYER: For all anyone knows, nothing is. Everything has to be taken on trust; truth is only that which is taken to be true. It's the currency of living. There may be nothing behind it, but it doesn't make any difference so long as it is honored. One acts on assumptions. What do you assume?

. . . Tom Stoppard (1966)

Glossary

AFRTS: Armed Forces Radio and Television Service

Aperture: an opening, hole, gap

ARVN: Army of the Republic of South Vietnam

AWOL: Absent without leave

Boot camp: a base dedicated to the basic training of recruits

BBC: British Broadcasting Corporation

C-130: four engine turboprop, military troop/cargo transport aircraft

CO: Commanding Officer or Company Commander, normally a captain or higher

Corpsmen: Naval enlisted, medical personnel

C-rations: box containing canned food, cigarettes, and accessory items

Flak jacket: sleeveless jacket made of dense fabric reinforced with protective Kevlar panels

Flechettes: metal, dart-like projectile

GI: *general issue* of clothing given new recruits. Hence, enlisted troops became known as GIs

G.I. Bill: law enacted by Congress providing benefits for military veterans, including college tuition assistance

Hamlet: a primitive settlement, generally two to four families. A cluster of hamlets make up a village

H & S: Headquarters & Service, a command company

HQ: battalion headquarters

ID: identification

Ka-bar: brand of military combat knifes

LSD: landing ship, docking

M67 Zippo: flame tank

MAG 16: Marine Corps Air Group 16

NCO: non-commissioned officer, corporal or sergeant

Pedicab: tricycle rickshaw providing transportation

Pfc: private first-class (one rank higher than private)

POW: prisoner of war

Punji stakes: sharpened wood or bamboo inserted into the ground point up

PX: Post Exchange, military department store; Air Force uses term, BX or Base Exchange

Seabee: heterograph for C.B., meaning naval "construction battalion"

Six-by: military transport truck with six-wheel drive

Uniform Code of Military Justice (UCMJ): Federal law governing the military justice system

USO: United Service Organization

Viet Cong: Vietnamese communist, guerrilla fighters called VC

Water Buffalo (military): a portable water tank mounted on two wheels

Suggested Readings

Boot, Max. *The Road Not Taken: Edward Lansdale and the American Tragedy in Vietnam.* Liveright, 2018.

Caputo, Philip. *A Rumor of War.* Holt Paperbacks, 1996.

Fitzgerald, Frances. *Fire in the Lake: The Vietnamese and the Americans in Vietnam.* Little Brown and Company, 1972.

Halberstam, David. *The Best and the Brightest.* Random House, Inc., 1972.

Halberstam, David. *The Making of a Quagmire: America and Vietnam During the Kennedy Era.*

Roman & Littlefield Publishers, (revised edition) 2007.

Herr, Michael. *Dispatches.* Vintage Books, (revised edition) 1991.

Logevall, Fredrik. *Choosing War.* University of California Press, 1999.

McMaster, H. R. *Dereliction of Duty*, HarperCollins Publishers, 1997.

Ninh, Bao, *The Sorrow of War*, Vintage Books, 2005.

Sheehan, Neil. *A Bright Shining Lie.* Vintage, 2009.

Suggested Documentaries

BBC Broadcast: *My Lai Tapes*. BBC Radio World Service, 2008.

Burns, Ken & Novick, Lynn: *The Vietnam War*. PBS, 2017.

Davis, Neil: *Frontline*. Austrailan Screen on NFSA Website, 1979.

Davis, Peter: *Hearts and Minds*. The Criterion Collection, 1974.

Nguyen, Ho: *The Chu Chi Tunnels*. Mickey Grant Films, 1991.

Taylor, David C.: *The Spy in the Hanoi Hilton*. Smithsonian Channel, 2015.

Sonneborn, Barbara: *Regret to Inform*. PBS, 1998.

Winterfilm Collective: *The Winter Soldier*. Orsen Welles Cinema, 1972.

About the Author

E. A. Cooper served in the U.S. Marine Corps (1962-1966). Upon his return to civilian life, he earned an associate's degree in general education from Birdwood Junior College in Thomasville, Georgia (1968); a bachelor's degree in education (speech & drama major) from Georgia Southwestern College in Americus, Georgia (1971); and then attended The University of Georgia in Athens, Georgia where he pursued a master's program in journalism (radio, TV, & film major) and earned a doctorate degree in adult education (1977).

After completion of his formal studies, Dr. Cooper served in the position of Director of Continuing Education and later Dean of Evening Administration with Albany Technical College in Albany, Georgia. He retired in 2014. Other books by Dr. Cooper include: *B.C. Street, Vietnam By The Light of the Moon, The Okinawa We Lost, and The Longleaf Pine Murder.*